GURU DUTT

A LIFE IN CINEMA

Nasreen Munni Kabir

OXFORD
UNIVERSITY PRESS

OXFORD
UNIVERSITY PRESS

YMCA Library Building, Jai Singh Road, New Delhi 110 001

Oxford University Press is a department of the University of Oxford. It furthers the University's objective of excellence in research, scholarship, and education by publishing worldwide in

Oxford New York

Athens Auckland Bangkok Bogota Buenos Aires Calcutta Cape Town Chennai Dar es Salaam Delhi Florence Hong Kong Istanbul Karachi Kuala Lumpur Madrid Melbourne Mexico City Mumbai Nairobi Paris São Paolo Shanghai Singapore Taipei Tokyo Toronto Warsaw

with associated companies in Berlin Ibadan

Published in India
By Oxford University Press, New Delhi

Oxford India Paperbacks 1997
Second impression 2000

ISBN 019 564274 0

Typeset by Rupert Snell
Printed in India by Pauls Press, New Delhi 110 020
Published by Manzar Khan, Oxford University Press
YMCA Library Building, Jai Singh Road, New Delhi 110 001

GURU DUTT

CONTENTS

Preface

Since the late 1970s when I first began programming Indian films for festivals and television in Europe, it became clear to me that Guru Dutt's films were the most engaging of the Hindi cinema selection and were equalled only by the enigmatic and often tragic character that he himself assumed on screen. I soon discovered that I was far from being the only one struck by Guru Dutt and by the special lyricism that haunts his films; there were thousands of people — both young and old — who never hesitated to quote his name when asked to recall a favourite director. Curtains billowing in the breeze, papers flying in the air like the last flutter of autumn leaves, a lonely figure moving discreetly between light and shade — these images continue to stir countless people for whom Guru Dutt's art remains a vital living force more than three decades after his death.

Some years later, in 1987, when I was making a Channel 4 documentary series on Hindi cinema titled *Movie Mahal*, a special feature on Guru Dutt was a natural choice. Though Guru Dutt had died several years earlier (and his wife Geeta had died on July 20, 1972), I was lucky enough to get to know many members of his immediate family. My first encounter with his son Tarun had taken place in 1982, and when I met him again to talk about the Channel 4 documentary, he was happy to help with film excerpts and information. Tarun so resembled his father — especially when he smiled with that familiar half-smile of Preetam or Kalu — that it made Guru Dutt's absence be felt even more acutely. The research for *In Search of Guru Dutt* (1989), the resulting three-part documentary, involved extensive interviews with Guru Dutt's family, friends and with many of the people who had worked most closely with him during his tragically short life: excerpts from those interviews, together with extensive clips from Guru Dutt's films, provided the substance of *In Search of Guru Dutt*. The title for the documentary came from an experience when visiting Guru Dutt's uncle, B.B. Benegal, one evening in 1986. As I started walking up the three flights of stairs to his studio in Calcutta, the lights went out, leaving me in the darkness. On all fours, I groped my way up each step thinking to myself that the final programme just had to be called 'In Search of Guru Dutt'. When I finally arrived at Mr Benegal's door, he opened it and shone his flashlight in my eyes and said, 'Where's your torch? This is Calcutta, you know!'

The most frustrating part of those years of research was knowing that Guru Dutt himself would never speak of his films or his life. The cruel irony of belated recognition has visited itself on many artists, and if we think of the posthumous recognition of the poet Vijay of *Pyaasa*, it could be said that Guru Dutt had a premonition of being among such artists; indeed, his contribution to Indian cinema has only been fully recognized some years after his death in 1964. In this respect the words of John Berger, in his book *About Looking* (Pantheon Books, New York 1980) on the life and work of the Italian sculptor Giacometti, strike one as applying so very closely to Guru Dutt also:

> Every artist's work changes when he dies. And finally no one remembers what his work was like when he was alive. Sometimes one can read what his contemporaries had to say about it. The difference of emphasis and interpretation is largely a question of historical development. But the death of the artist is also the dividing line... The reason Giacometti's death seems to have changed his work so radically is that his work had so much to do with an awareness of death. It is as though his death confirms his work: as though one could now arrange his works in a line leading to his death, which would constitute far more than the interruption or termination of that line which would, on the contrary, constitute the starting point for reading back along that line for appreciating his life's work.

Over the past few years, I have felt that some of the interview material collected during my research on Guru Dutt should be made available in print because it comprises a valuable record of his life through the testimonies of his contemporaries — a generation whose own histories are inseparable from Guru Dutt's story. That idea lay behind the writing of this book, in which I have tried to follow Guru Dutt's career through his films, this biographical narrative being side-lit by the memories of those closest to him. The result is not a full biography, but rather a memoir and a tribute to one who was variously seen and loved as director, fellow-actor, colleague, brother, father, son or artistic mentor.

Sadly, since 1985, many of those I interviewed have passed away — among them B.B. Benegal, Pandit Narendra Sharma, Tarun Dutt, Raj Khosla, R.D. Burman and Atmaram; and this further reminder of the uncertainty of existence underlines the importance of preserving reminiscences and perspectives.

The generosity with which Guru Dutt's family and colleagues have shared their precious memories has made this work possible. My first acknowledgement must therefore be to all those whose conversations form the heart of this book: the help of Abrar Alvi, V.K. Murthy, S. Guruswamy, Johnny Walker, Waheeda Rehman, Kaifi Azmi, Majrooh Sultanpuri, Shyam Benegal, Dev Anand, Mohan Sehgal, Satyavati Gopalan, Mehmood, Y.G. Chawhan and Tanuja was essential to the writing of Guru Dutt's life. I would also like to thank all Guru Dutt's family, including his now deceased mother Vasanthi Padukone, his three brothers Devi Dutt, Vijay Padukone and the late Atmaram, his elder son the late Tarun Dutt, and his younger son Arun Dutt who was so generous with his time and in allowing me use of a wealth of photographs from his own collection. I am particularly indebted to Guru Dutt's sister Lalitha Lajmi, who has collected materials and photographs for me over the years and has always encouraged me in this endeavour.

I would also like to thank Filmfare, the National Film Archives of India, Poona, and the many friends who have contributed in other ways to the project: Gopal Gandhi, Peter Chappell, Urvashi Butalia, Khalid Mohammed, P.K. Nair, Wolf Suschitzky, Anil Tejani, and the late Uday Row Kavi.

My special thanks go to my husband Rupert Snell who so carefully edited this book, and who never failed to spur me on.

CHAPTER ONE

The Padukone Family

Surrounded by her large family, Guru Dutt's frail mother, Vasanthi Padukone, celebrated her eighty-fifth birthday in 1993 in a small rented ground-floor flat in Matunga, a middle-class residential area in Bombay. The Matunga flat had become home for the Padukones in 1942 when they moved there after living for several years in Calcutta. The Padukone household included a maternal grandmother and five children: Guru Dutt, Atmaram, Lalitha, Devi and Vijay. Little money and a closed living space were both very much part of Guru Dutt's early years in Bombay when, uncomplainingly, he slept on a bed placed on the patio that extended out into the common courtyard. Vasanthi Padukone's eighty-fifth birthday photographs show her now-grown children standing proudly by their respective sons, daughters and smiling grandchildren. On any other day of the year, it is usually the sounds of Mrs Padukone's more energetic neighbours that fill these two modest rooms in which there is little escape from a lifetime of memories.

Originally from Mangalore, Vasanthi Padukone's family lived in Burma for a few years and there, in 1908, Vasanthi was born. Her parents returned to India when she was three years old as her grandfather was dying. A few years later, Vasanthi's father was cheated by a business partner and was forced to sell the family home. Her parents began to live separately, and her father, whom she loved dearly, lived in Bombay and Poona, never managing to retain a steady job. Vasanthi Padukone had an unsettled and unhappy childhood, moving from Udipi to Bombay, from Bombay to Secunderabad, and from Secunderabad to Madras — from the home of one relative to another. As was the common practice in those days, when Vasanthi was only twelve, her mother arranged her marriage to Shivshankar Rao Padukone, a college friend of Vasanthi's brother Ramanath. Ramanath lived in Kasargod but studied in Madras.

Both Guru Dutt's parents belonged to Mangalore's Saraswat community — a Brahmin caste originally from North India which had settled in different parts of the country. Their caste name is traditionally associated with the Saraswati river of Kashmir, though many Saraswats live in the coastal districts near Goa. The Konkani-speaking Saraswat community of Mangalore boasts many scholars and artists. Shivshankar Padukone was from a modest but educated family, and was himself studying for his B.A. degree when he married at the age of twenty. He had nine elder brothers and three sisters and was the youngest son of the thirteen children. His mother had died when he was only thirteen. Most of the Padukones had married within the extended family and Vasanthi was the only outsider. When Vasanthi reached puberty, the nuptial ceremony was performed. Soon after that the young couple moved to Panambur, a village near Mangalore where Shivshankar worked as a headmaster in a school run by the village Panchayat. A year or so later, in 1924, Shivshankar moved to Bangalore where he began to work in a bank. Vasanthi and her mother joined him there, and in 1925, during the rainy season in July, Guru Dutt was born.

Though some seventy years have passed since the birth of her first child, Vasanthi Padukone's love for Guru Dutt has only increased. Everything connected with his life is given more importance than the events in her own life, or in the lives of her other children. Even if Vasanthi Padukone were to choose a respite from the past, living in the Matunga flat would make that difficult. Every part of the flat evokes vivid memories. She remembers that Balraj Sahni worked here in this room on the dialogues for her son's first film; and Guru Dutt sat at that wooden table near the window while writing the story of *Pyaasa*. The plainness of the table is hidden by the beauty of the sunlight streaming through the pale green cotton curtains that cover the iron bars of the window. A black-and-white enlarged photograph of Guru Dutt in his *Pyaasa* role hangs in a simple wooden frame from the wall of his mother's room. The photograph is adorned by a garland, flowers for the dead.

VASANTHI PADUKONE: I was only twelve years old when I was married. I didn't know anything about life. I was sixteen when Guru Dutt was born. Before his birth, an astrologer had predicted that I would have a son who would become world famous; he would be a good man and take care of the whole family. I was so young — I hadn't had any children then — so I felt embarrassed, and didn't ask the astrologer many questions. Guru Dutt was born on July 9, 1925 at noon; the nurse said he weighed less than 6lbs. The day that he was born, he was the only boy amongst seven girls born that day in the hospital in Bangalore. When Guru Dutt was only a month old he used to smile whenever he saw anyone. As a young child, Guru Dutt was very naughty and stubborn; he was very short-tempered too. He had a habit of asking question after question. I used to go mad answering his questions; but he wouldn't leave me alone until I answered him.

In a memoir published in *Imprint* in 1979, Vasanthi Padukone elaborated on Guru Dutt's childhood, recounting the events that followed her return home with her eleven day old infant:

On the twelfth day, the cradle ceremony was performed. A few relatives and neighbours were invited. My elder brother [Vitthal] had suggested two names for my son: 'Vasanth Kumar' and 'Gurudutt' because the baby was born on Thursday ['the day of the guru']... On Guru Dutt's second birthday [in 1927], I dressed him in red clothes which were his favourites, put his ornaments on and sent him to the landlord's place to wish them. It was midday when he returned home running; he fell near a well. He was hurt severely on the forehead. I took him to the nearby doctor. At night, he had high fever which continued for two weeks... We sat near the child by turns. By God's grace, the critical period was over. He uttered, 'Amma.' I gave him water from a spoon which he drank slowly. From a distance, I could hear Swami Samarth Ramdas' *shloka* sung by someone on the road by our house:

Who is the most happy in the world?
Ask your own mind to find out;
O mind, is it you who are responsible for whatever you suffer?

Some people said that Guru had fallen ill because the spirit of a man who had died by falling in the well had come upon him. So, we called the *mantravadi* to remove the evil spirit. He told us that the child should not be called by the name Vasanth Kumar, which was the first name that we had given him. Since then he was called Gurudutt.

In 1927, when Mahatma Gandhi visited Bangalore, Vasanthi Padukone was deeply moved by his teachings. Vasanthi wrote to Gandhiji saying that she wanted to leave her husband and young son and join his ashram. Gandhiji wrote back dissuading her, and said that her duty lay in family life, and in raising her son so that he might be of good and strong character. Shivshankar Padukone resigned once again from his bank job and moved to Mangalore, while his wife visited her cousin in Calcutta for a short while with her young son, Guru Dutt. Shivshankar was then appointed Manager of the Sadananda Cooperative Printing Press in Mangalore that published the Kannada weekly, *Rashtrabandhu*.

Vasanthi Padukone, like her own parents, had an unhappy marriage. The lack of understanding and communication with her husband seemed to worsen as time went by. Her accounts of those early years of marriage reflected her restlessness, and showed a need to escape from the reality of her life. In 1928, Vasanthi learnt that her father had died in Bombay at the J.J. Hospital. What particularly upset her was that he had died with no family member by his side; she had wanted to see him some months before but could not afford the train fare. When Vasanthi was expecting her second child, her husband resigned from his job at the printing press. On Vasanthi's request, her brother, Ramanath, who had moved from Madras, sent her money to visit him in Ahmedabad. In an article printed in *Eve's Weekly* in June 20-26, 1987, Vasanthi Padukone describes her stay at her brother's home:

> Ramanath received us, but not very warmly. His financial position was not good, and he had his own problems. His wife had been very ill and was therefore very weak. When they found out that I was in the family way, it added to their hostility to us. This was in December 1928. Ramanath's adopted uncle used to suffer from bouts of insanity. This caused the insane man to howl. Watching all this, Guru Dutt used to feel frightened and cling to me. He'd beg, 'Ma, let us go somewhere else.'

They left for Calcutta soon after this incident. Shivshankar Padukone joined them there, first finding work as a salesman, and then as an administrative clerk at the Burmah Shell Company where he was to work for thirty years. In 1929, Vasanthi Padukone gave birth to her second son, Shashidhar, who died when he was only seven months old. Vasanthi remembers how Shashidhar's death had traumatized Guru Dutt. He suffered from a high temperature for several days following the death of his little brother. The Padukones moved to a flat on Paddapukur Road, and in 1930, Vasanthi had a third son, Atmaram, followed by the birth of their only daughter, Lalitha, in 1932. The Padukones had two other children, Devi (born in 1938) and Vijay (born in 1941). From Paddapukur Road, they moved to a flat in Ashton Road and then to Bolai Mansions in Bhowanipur. Next to the house in Bhowanipur was an open space where Bengali *jatras* (dramas staged by roving players) were performed. Guru Dutt would never miss a performance and had by that time learnt to speak Bengali. To amuse his young siblings, Guru Dutt would powder his face, tie a cloth around him like a dhoti or a sari, and imitate the actors he had seen.

VASANTHI PADUKONE: I remember when Uday Shankar's troupe performed in Bombay in 1935 [Vasanthi Padukone and Guru Dutt had travelled to Bombay for a brief holiday]; I was going to see the performance and Guru Dutt said he wanted to go with me. I said no. He became very angry and didn't eat for three days. When I promised to take him with me, then he ate. He vowed that one day he would perform on stage. I just took it as child's talk.

In Calcutta, Guru Dutt used to watch the *jatras* all night long — the *Mahabharat*, *Ramayan* and so on. If there was a puppet show on anywhere he used to go to watch. He read a lot: day and night he used to have a book with him. He didn't have any academic qualifications, but he gained so much knowledge. Whatever Guru Dutt wanted to do, he had to do.

Before Guru Dutt was five years old he had accompanied his mother on her travels, from Bangalore to Calcutta, from Calcutta to Mangalore via Madras, from Mangalore to Ahmedabad, and finally from Ahmedabad back to Calcutta. The early travels with his mother may have been exciting for the young Guru Dutt; but they were unsettling as well. It was in Calcutta that his parents, brother (Atmaram), and sister (Lalitha), lived together at last, and despite their continued financial difficulties, their home had a semblance of family life in which childhood and adolescence could take their natural course. Guru Dutt's later attachment to the city reveals his sense of well-being there; this attachment was clearly not only intellectual but also emotional and even spiritual.

For Vasanthi Padukone, Calcutta meant less isolation because she could rely on the financial and moral support of her cousin, B.B. Benegal, who was also a great influence on the Padukone children. Benegal had lived all his life in Calcutta, mostly in the crowded area around Dharamtalla Street. Even in his seventies, he worked long hours designing and painting cinema hoardings; and though he would never be recognized as an important artist — his work was mainly confined to commercial art — he was always confident of his own talent. Benegal's painting of a young half-clad man with a snake coiled around his body particularly impressed Guru Dutt and he even composed a snake dance number inspired by his uncle's painting. B.B. Benegal's most important influence on the Padukone family lay in the fact that he understood the nature of creative people and had in his own life been able to survive as an artist.

B.B. BENEGAL: The family came to Calcutta in 1929. Guru Dutt was only four years old; he looked like a beautiful doll. His father got a job as a journalist and then he worked at Burmah Shell; he had two jobs. He was a very good journalist but due to their difficult circumstances, he was rather frustrated. He could not achieve what he wanted. It was hard for him to fight, because of the lack of resources, the many family troubles, and because of the children who were being born nearly every two years. So he was frustrated, naturally. Vasanthi was one of my dearest cousins, so I offered my meagre help. At that time, in 1931, I had just opened my studio. I helped as much I could — that was not very much. This went on until the war started in 1939. To make ends meet, Vasanthi gave private tuition in Canarese [Kannada] or Hindi or in whatever language she could. She used to get a little money while her mother looked after the children. I told Vasanthi to send her children to my home whenever she felt like it; I told her, 'Leave Guru Dutt to me, I will look after him.' I put him in David Hare's school which was run by the Jesuits. Before that, he was at a South Indian school where he was not doing very well. When he started studying in an English medium school, he was quite happy. He did well, and passed in every subject; he was a good student. In the meantime, I could see that he had a lot of intuition for creative work. I could see from the way that he moved. He was very good in the house. He would tell my wife, 'Let us do this in this way.' Sometimes he would take my camera. I would tell him not to use it; but then he would ask my wife and take it from her. I was very strict about the camera. Later Guru Dutt bought me a 16mm Bellard Bolex from London and presented it to me.

I could see that he had an intuition for dance, and he used to love music. I had a beautiful HMV deluxe model gramophone with an exhibition sound box; in fact I still have it now. He used to play S.D. Burman's music — not film music but folk music. Guru Dutt loved S.D. Burman. [Music director S.D.Burman had started composing and recording music, including film music for the Bengali cinema from 1939, and only moved to Bombay in 1944].

There was a five-year age difference between Guru Dutt and his brother Atmaram who, being the quiet one in childhood, had to contend with a boisterous elder brother. Vasanthi Padukone remembers Guru Dutt being very fond of his brother. Atmaram, on the other hand, was made aware that it was Guru Dutt who was his mother's favourite. When Atmaram was in his twenties, he worked as Guru Dutt's assistant on four films (*Baaz*, *Jaal*, *Aar Paar*, and *Mr & Mrs 55)* and later produced *Baharen Phir Bhi Aayengi.* When Guru Dutt died, Atmaram had made a twenty-minute documentary on Guru Dutt called *Shraddhanjali* (Tribute). The short film includes many stills of Guru Dutt on various film locations, and features a number of film excerpts with a commentary by Abrar Alvi. In later life, Atmaram became a director and producer in his own right, and worked from his offices at the Natraj Studio in Andheri — a short distance from Guru Dutt's old studios where *Chaudhvin ka Chand* and *Sahib Bibi aur Ghulam* were filmed. The large stage originally built for Alexander Korda (who was planning to make 'Taj Mahal' — a film project which was later shelved); was converted into a studio in 1956 by Guru Dutt. The Guru Dutt Studios building was pulled down in the late sixties, since it was right in the middle of what was to become Bombay's Highway no.4.

Atmaram's office, like all the other rooms in which Guru Dutt's family and friends spend much of their time, is dominated by a black-and-white photographic portrait of Guru Dutt. Atmaram has always been a gentle and quiet person; he speaks of his brother with contained emotion:

> We came from a lower middle-class family, so there was a lot of ambition to do well. Success was very important; it was very necessary to do things in life. My mother fired that ambition. Guru Dutt wasn't the top of the class at school; he was bright — he finished his matriculation — but he never went to college. He spoke Hindi very well, but he was more at home in English and in Bengali. At home we spoke Konkani but a lot of English too. He thought in English and wrote in English and that's the truth. Look at the notes in his scripts.
>
> Guru Dutt read so widely; that was my father's influence. My father had studied English literature. When we were young Guru Dutt was very active, he played a lot. He had a group of friends around him including two neighbours, Naveen and Ratilal; I always wanted to go with him and he would leave me behind. His early days were very lively, full of mischief. We were strict vegetarians at home; my grandmother did most of the cooking. One day, Guru Dutt brought a couple of eggs and made an omelette while my

grandmother was away at the bazaar; he loved cooking. When my grandmother came back and smelt the eggs, all hell was let loose.

Guru Dutt's only sister, Lalitha Lajmi, is a well-known painter and artist. She lives with her husband, Captain Gopalkrishna Lajmi, in Lokhandwala Complex in Andheri, a suburb of Bombay. She has two children: a daughter, Kalpana, who is a film-maker, and a son, Devdas, who has followed his father's career in the Merchant Navy. Lalitha's own artistic sensitivity increased the awe she felt for her elder brother. Guru Dutt lives on in her mind and in her thoughts. On a table in the room where she paints stands a small framed photograph of Guru Dutt. It is not a still from a film but is one of the many family photographs that Lalitha cherishes. In this black-and-white photograph Guru Dutt is seen wearing his much-needed glasses (he had very poor eyesight); and his face is in profile as he looks far into the distance. From an old file that Lalitha treasures, falls a letter that Guru Dutt once wrote to her; his handwriting is large and slanted.

Lalitha remarks how impressions and experiences in one's own life return transformed in one's work. Each of the Padukones' feelings for Calcutta lives on. Lalitha points to an early painting showing the confining walls of a roof terrace, typical of the architecture of Calcutta, and adds that Guru Dutt used a similar background for the *Pyaasa* song, *Aaj sajan mohe ang laga lo:*

> Wherever you are, those environments do play a great role in your life, especially if you are a creative person. I think these things do matter. Our Calcutta house was very small: one bedroom, one living room and a kitchen in the middle. My mother used to teach in a school and so my grandmother cooked for us. We would sit on the floor and eat in the middle room. In the other room, my grandmother used to do her puja; she would light a lamp and say her prayers every evening. There was a wall on one side of the room where Guru Dutt used to do shadow play; in the light of the lamp he would create a performance with his fingers and hands.
>
> My uncle, Mr Benegal, was a great influence on us; he was a fascinating man. He was also an artist, a commercial artist, and he used to paint many of the film hoardings in Calcutta. My uncle had a large studio, and downstairs were his living quarters. We used to spend many weekends at his house. He lived in one of those old buildings, next to one of the oldest cinemas in Calcutta, the Jyoti Cinema, on Dharamtalla Street. My father was only a clerk in Burmah Shell so we couldn't afford to go and see films, but my

uncle would get free passes, so there were times we may have seen two or three films in a day — both foreign and Indian films.

I remember Guru Dutt was very fond of keeping parrots. He would talk to them, and early each morning he would feed them; he was very fond of paper kites too, and loved making Diwali sparklers. He used to make the sparklers in the little outhouse that we had. In those days, in Calcutta, Baul singers performed on the streets. I remember that we never gave them coins, but a handful of rice. They would walk by our house in Bhowanipur, walking along with their *ektara* and singing devotional songs. Guru Dutt has used the Baul style of singing in *Pyaasa*, but he has picturized instead a woman singing *'aaj sajan mohe'* whereas in Calcutta the Baul singers are usually men. Before we moved to Bhowanipur, we lived in a small flat in a building called Bolai Mansions which was very close to a Kali temple. We went there often to see the *puja*. Probably these events must have influenced Guru Dutt, because a lot of the past, of those days, has come into his films, especially in *Pyaasa*.

Vasanthi Padukone, determined to acquire the education that she had missed as a child, passed her matriculation exam in 1940 a year before Guru Dutt passed his in 1941. Finances were still a great problem, and finding a way to supplement the family income was more pressing than acquiring further education. At sixteen, Guru Dutt got his first job as a telephone operator in a mill on a monthly salary of Rs 40. Atmaram and Lalitha remember that with his first salary their brother bought presents for all the family.

Guru Dutt spent most of his free time with his older cousin and friend, Sudarshan Benegal (who was studying art), photographing the animals in the zoo or the plants in Calcutta's botanical gardens. Guru Dutt never failed to find great encouragement in the Benegal household.

B.B. BENEGAL: He got inspiration from my painting called 'The Struggle for Existence' [the painting showing a man holding a snake coiled around his body]. I had painted it during my student days and I received an award for it. When Guru Dutt saw the painting, he said, 'Uncle, I feel like dancing to this.' He didn't know how to dance; but somehow he made up that snake-charmer dance. He invented it. He performed the same dance in front of our Saraswat Association, and got good applause, so he was inspired. His actions were so beautiful, smooth, and at the same time direct, impulsive. You can see that he's playing with the snake, he's trying to hold it, and the snake is trying to get away. He showed us such a beautiful thing. I first saw his dance in Eden Garden. Then I told him, 'Tomorrow, I'm going to film you on colour film.' Guru Dutt and I went to Eden Garden early next morning, there was a beautiful sun rising. It was in November. He put my red shawl on his head and tied a yellow cloth around his waist. He said, 'Uncle, give me some make-up'; and I did. He looked just like a snake charmer. There was no music playing as he was dancing; he was just *thinking* the music.

B.B. Benegal's painting of the man and the snake has its ambiguities; although the title of the work, 'The Struggle for Existence', suggests a combat, Guru Dutt's interpretation of the painting is recalled as being playful and fearless. The snake dance was performed at a gathering for the Saraswat community of Calcutta and was Guru Dutt's first public appearance on stage. Atmaram remembers that Guru Dutt received a gift of Rs 5 from an impressed friend, Mr Bhandarkar, who many years later became the Bombay distributor for Guru Dutt Productions' 1956 film, *C.I.D.*

B.B. BENEGAL: He was barely fifteen years old when he said to me, 'Uncle, I want you to introduce me to Uday Shankar.' At that time, Uday Shankar was in Calcutta. I said, 'You fool, have you gone crazy? Just because I know him — whatever for?' He said, 'I want to join his Dance Centre at Almora.' I told him not to be silly and to wait; he said 'No, I want to go.' He secretly gave an audition to Uday Shankar through the help of some friends. Somehow Guru Dutt danced that same snake dance before Uday Shankar, who was crazy over him. The next day, Guru Dutt said, 'Uncle, I saw Uday Shankar.' 'You saw Uday Shankar? What did he say?'; 'He said, "Come to Almora".'

So I went and talked to Uday Shankar; I was responsible for designing their souvenirs, advertisements, everything. Uday Shankar said he had no objection to Guru Dutt joining, but the Centre's administrator, Mr Burse, had to agree. The Almora Centre was sponsored by Americans; George Burse was an American too. I asked my friend Hemmad [a leading film distributor in Calcutta who was also a Saraswat Brahmin] to talk to Burse who said, 'Let him come, we will look after him free.' The family couldn't afford the fees anyway. I remember when Guru Dutt heard he had been accepted at Almora, he jumped like hell; then I gave him a few blankets and some money. I said, 'Take the blankets because it is very cold in Almora. If you have any difficulties, just write to me.' In those days, I was living at 183, Dharamtalla Street; we stayed there from 1931 to 1943. Guru Dutt first worked at a mill. He only worked there for a month and a half. He didn't even collect his last pay. The Marwari chap working there said to me, 'What is the matter? Your nephew never even took his money. Where has he run off to?' I said, 'He hasn't run off, he's gone to Almora.'

CHAPTER TWO

Early Years

With the help of B.B. Benegal and a family friend, Mr S.R. Hemmad, Guru Dutt won a five-year scholarship of Rs 75 a month to study at the Uday Shankar India Culture Centre in Almora. Uday Shankar's father was a *diwan* (minister) in the service of the Maharajah of Jhalawar (between Kota and Ujjain). When he retired, a pension permitted the family to live in Benaras while Uday Shankar moved to London with his father who practiced law but also staged musical productions in the mid-twenties. Uday Shankar had initially wanted to be a painter, and studied at the Royal College of Art in London; but soon his passion for dance overtook his other interests. He lived in London for ten years, during which period he worked for a while with the celebrated Russian ballerina, Anna Pavlova. In 1929, Uday Shankar returned to India to form a troupe of dancers and musicians whom he took back to Europe to live and perform in Paris. The troupe included his younger brother, Ravi Shankar.

In 1938, Uday Shankar returned to India to stay, and realized his dream of opening a cultural centre for the performing arts. Uday Shankar's Centre attracted many talented musicians such as the great Ustad Allaudin Khan together with two promising disciples: his own son, Ali Akbar Khan, and Ravi Shankar, who both spent a short time at Almora. Many talented dancers also worked at the Centre, including Simkie from France and Uday Shankar's wife, Amala. Madame Simkie is well known in Bombay for having choreographed the magnificent dream sequence in Raj Kapoor's *Awaara* (1951). The style of dancing in this dream sequence is clearly inspired by Uday Shankar's own choreography in his film *Kalpana* (1948). In Ravi Shankar's autobiography titled *My Music, My Life* (Jonathan Cape, London 1969), Ravi Shankar describes his brother's Centre:

Uday started this culture center on almost twenty acres of land, and he constructed modern studios for dance, drama and music, with built-in stages, costume rooms, workshops and rehearsal halls. He brought in the best known *gurus* of India, among them Shankaran Namboodri, the greatest living *Kathakali* dancer, from whom Dada (Uday Shankar) received his own dancing training and the only real *guru* Dada ever had in his life. There were also Kandappan Pillai, one of the notable *Bharatanatyam* teachers, *Manipuri guru* Amobi Sinha, and even Allaudin Khan to supervise instrumental music. The center was an ideal combination of the old *ashram* type of school plus the modern workshop atmosphere one finds in some of the open-air institutions of the West. The teachers and students were all very close, and Uday, with his magnetism and strong personality, kept the entire complex functioning.

The India Culture Centre attracted students from all over India, and Uday Shankar made sure that it was also possible for students of modest means like Guru Dutt to join. Uday Shankar's main criterion of selection was that a student should be genuinely interested in dance. Many students at Almora became well-known artists in their own right, not only in dance but also in other disciplines. Mohan Schgal, who was to become a reputed film director and producer, was one of Guru Dutt's contemporaries at Uday Shankar's Centre.

MOHAN SEHGAL: Guru Dutt was a year senior to me at Almora. Although he initially joined films as a choreographer, I think that was merely in order to have an opening in the industry. Guru Dutt was not a good dancer, but he knew the technique. Uday Shankar often said that his aim was not only to produce dancers, but all-round artists. Shankar would say, 'I want to develop your creative faculties so that you can be better human beings.' Our classes were taken by specialists in many fields. Sumitranandan Pant, a leading Hindi mystic poet, taught us literature; Professor Mattrani gave lectures in psychology. There was an emphasis on all-round mental development, not just in one dance form or another. The accent was on creativity. We were given situations around which we had to create a dance that would then be criticised by our colleagues. Uday Shankar would always say, 'You must get a grounding in a specific tradition, and later on when you are creating, do not think of technique, think of expression. If you want to create something in a pure school of dance, you can. But if you want to give expression to a modern idea, then forget all the dance forms that you have learnt. They will come to you automatically because you have digested them, they are in your subconscious.'

Like Mohan Sehgal, the celebrated dancer Satyavati Gopalan was greatly influenced by Uday Shankar's teachings, and had joined the Centre in 1941. Satyavati Gopalan is now in her seventies; she lives alone in an immaculately tidy, two-roomed apartment in Colaba, Bombay. Her voice becomes charged with life as she leafs through her treasured album, whose faded black-and-white photographs bring back the old Almora days:

> The classes took place in the main studio; there were about fifty students. Shankar used to tell us, 'If you don't know how to dance, all the better because I can teach you my style, my way.' He started the class by giving us a rhythm, and we walked to that rhythm. He sat in a corner and watched the position of our bodies, and the position of our arms. Then using the movement of the arms, he would tell us to make a small movement to a certain beat. From this small movement, we developed a bigger movement. From a big movement to one big pose. Then he would get us to work on expression. Not a stylized kind of expression. He would say, 'Show me anger, show me love, show me a smile, show me shyness.' Some of us did not know what to do with ourselves. Shankar would say, 'Do what you like, but just do.' That was his idea — just do.
>
> Guru Dutt joined us at the end of 1941 or possibly in early 1942 — I forget. He spoke fluent Bengali because he had lived in Calcutta before that. Uday Shankar liked him and lent him his camera because Guru Dutt knew how to use it properly, and he could be seen taking photographs all the time. I think Guru Dutt was easily the most handsome young man at the Centre. All eyes were on him. But he was so unassuming, and shy too. He could wear any colour and look nice. He had beautiful jet black hair, and a very calm face; a calm face but there was a lot within him. He never spoke much, and if he did, he sounded like a young child. He had that sort of innocence.
>
> I remember the Ram Lila rehearsals. Sachin Shankar [Uday Shankar's cousin] played Rama and Guru Dutt was Lakshman. Guru Dutt was so humble, so unassuming, and being such a shy boy himself, he looked natural as Lakshman. We all had to take part in the Ram Lila; I played three roles. During the week we performed, all the villagers came to watch. Uday Shankar wanted the play to have a natural setting. Just imagine the scene: we came down the hillside with the Himalayas as a background, wearing our

costumes, and holding burning torches in our hands. The whole procession walked passed the villagers who would cry out, 'Jai Ram, Jai Sita, Jai Lakshman!' The drums were beating as we marched to the stage and took our places behind a huge, white screen. The whole drama was then performed as a shadow play. Uday Shankar had visited Indonesia, Bali and Java, and had seen similar plays, so he wanted to create a shadow play too. It is the most difficult thing to do, adjusting the lights to make your figure appear small or large and looming. Shankar's Ram Lila was beautiful, especially the scene in which Hanuman becomes small and then large again. Everyone clapped. Such a memory.

While Guru Dutt enjoyed the creative environment of Almora, his mother, brothers and sister had left Calcutta in January 1942 as rumours of imminent bombing by the Japanese spread in the city. Vasanthi Padukone took her children to stay with her brother-in-law, Swami Ramdas, who had an ashram called 'Anandashram' in Kanhangad, South India (Karnataka). Shivshankar Padukone stayed on in Calcutta but when Burmah Shell decided to move their offices to Bombay, Shivshankar agreed to be transferred. When he had managed to rent an apartment, his wife and children joined him in Bombay on August 9, 1942, the day when the 'Do or Die' agitation of the Quit India movement had started. Vasanthi Padukone supplemented the family income by teaching at Sitaram Poddar School. She was also writing short stories and translating Bengali novels into Kannada. Somehow, Vasanthi managed to send Guru Dutt Rs 5 per month for his personal expenses in Almora.

In December 1942, Uday Shankar brought his stage creation, the shadow play version of the Ram Lila with Sachin Shankar and Guru Dutt to Bombay. The Padukones were thrilled and proud to see the seventeen year old Guru Dutt with his long, flowing hair among Uday Shankar and his dancers. Guru Dutt performed his own composition, *The Swan Dance* on stage with Sundari Shridharani. While the dance troupe was in Bombay, Guru Dutt lived in the family flat in Matunga. Each morning, he would garland Uday Shankar's photograph as a sign of reverence to his teacher before lending a helping hand around the house, or looking after his younger brother, Vijay. Uday Shankar's troupe performed in Gujarat, Uttar Pradesh, and Maharashtra until March 1943 before they returned to Almora where Guru Dutt spent a further year.

In the early forties, the Uday Shankar Culture Centre, together with IPTA (Indian Peoples' Theatre Association, a progressive and leftist theatre movement formed in 1942 and informally affiliated to the Communist Party of India) and Chetan Anand (who was associated with IPTA) applied to the government for a licence in a special category which made it possible for them to make three films despite wartime restrictions on film production. The result was three highly original films, which now constitute a fascinating record of the times: *Dharti ke Lal* (1946, produced by IPTA, based on a story by Krishen Chander and directed by K.A. Abbas), *Neecha Nagar* (1946, directed by Chetan Anand) and *Kalpana* (1948, choreographed and directed by Uday Shankar).

As a result of the war years, most of the foreign funding had stopped and the India Culture Centre had to close down. Many of Uday Shankar's students returned home, finding themselves suddenly thrown out of the protected world that Shankar had created. Sometime in 1944, Guru Dutt returned to Bombay accompanied by three of his Almora friends: Anandi, Moni and Ghanshyam. Despite the meagre resources of the now eight-member Padukone household, Guru Dutt insisted on offering his friends hospitality until they found another place to live two months later. With the Centre closed, Uday Shankar started work on *Kalpana*, which was to be four years in the making. The film, dedicated to Guru Sankaran Namboodri, provides an interesting insight into the way students were taught dance at the Centre, and into the philosophy that motivated Shankar. *Kalpana* (Imagination), made in Hindi, was shot at the Gemini Studios in Madras, and is the story of Udayan (played by Uday Shankar), a young man who dreams of opening a *kalakendra* (art centre) in the Himalayas. Basing the film on the Almora model, Uday Shankar juxtaposes the purity and dedication of artists with the corruption and selfishness of the wealthy. Udayan the young dreamer fails to achieve his ambitions, and comes to realize that there is no place in society for artists. Despite the film's weaknesses, especially in dialogue, *Kalpana* is an effective, surreal, dance fantasy showing a path that Indian cinema could have followed but never did.

Guru Dutt did not forget what he had learnt at Almora with Uday Shankar, nor did he forget his childhood years spent in Calcutta. Throughout his life, he remained connected to Bengali culture not only because he married Geeta Roy, but also through its music (for example his use of music directors S.D. Burman and Hemant Kumar), its literature (his film adaptation of the Bengali novel *Sahib Bibi aur Ghulam*), and, above all, its cinema, particularly through the work of director P.C. Barua. Barua distinguished himself in making social melodramas such as *Devdas* (1936), written by the Bengali novelist Sarat Chandra Chatterjee, and these stories of personal crises had a deep impact on Guru Dutt. Guru Dutt's later screen personae shared a similar psyche to that of Devdas. Guru Dutt would always be drawn to the culture of Bengal and to its people, just as he had been in his youth. The closing of Uday Shankar's Centre coincided with the end of Guru Dutt's adolescence; and his early months in Bombay were filled with apprehension.

Guru Dutt did not know what he could do next. It seemed clear that he did not want to continue studying dance. Once again, it was Guru Dutt's uncle, B.B. Benegal, who gave Guru Dutt a new direction, taking him to Poona to introduce him to a helpful friend, Baburao Pai. Pai was Chief Executive of the Prabhat Film Company and Studio, and later became responsible for distributing Prabhat's films through his company Famous Pictures. Guru Dutt had met Baburao Pai briefly when Pai once visited Uday Shankar in Almora to discuss a film project that never materialised. Through Baburao Pai's recommendation, Guru Dutt was employed on a three-year contract as a dance director at Prabhat. Coincidentally, Baburao Pai was also responsible for helping Dev Anand join Prabhat, a first contract in a long career in films.

Prabhat Film Company was originally founded in Kolhapur in 1929 by V.G. Damle, S. Fatehlal, S.V. Kulkarni, and V. Shantaram, who all moved to Poona in 1933 where they set up their lavish and well-equipped studios. Prabhat, New Theatres and Bombay Talkies were considered the most influential North Indian studios of the 1930s, each producing highly acclaimed films. Prabhat's trademark showing a young woman blowing a *tutari* (trumpet) heralded a glorious quarter-century of the company's existence until 1953 when the studio closed down. Prabhat is still remembered for creating classic screen dramas such as the devotional film *Sant Tukaram* (1936), the social films, *Duniya na Mane* (1937) and *Aadmi* (1939), and the historical *Ramshastri* (1944).

Though Prabhat had lost its most important member in 1941 when V. Shantaram moved to Bombay to form his own film company, Rajkamal Kalamandir, the studio still maintained its high standards, offering its employees opportunities to learn every aspect of film-making. Despite the fact that Guru Dutt was on the studio's pay-roll as a choreographer, he also worked as an assistant director, and even as an actor. Guru Dutt appeared in bit roles in a few B-grade Prabhat films, roles that were only noticed by his immediate family. Vasanthi

Padukone remembers how thrilled the family was to see him for the first time on screen among a group of dancers — their laughter soon turning to tears when the next scene required Guru Dutt in the role of Lachhman to be beaten up and tied to a pole. This early screen appearance was for *Lakhrani* (1945), a film in which Guru Dutt also worked as an assistant to director Vishram Bedekar. In another Prabhat production, *Chand* (1944), directed by D.D. Kashyap and starring Begum Para and Sapru, Guru Dutt allegedly had a small role as Lord Krishna. In *Hum Ek Hain* (1946), a film promoting national unity, directed by P.L. Santoshi, Guru Dutt choreographed dances to the music of Husnlal-Bhagatram as well as worked as assistant to the director.

During the years that Guru Dutt lived and worked in Poona, his closest friends were actors Dev Anand, Rehman and Ramsingh, and these friendships were important to him both on and off the set. His friendship with Rehman lasted many years, with Rehman being cast in Guru Dutt's most important films. Ramsingh, too, acted in Guru Dutt's early films, while Guru Dutt's friendship with Dev Anand led to a first break in film direction in 1951.

Dev Anand, who started modestly at Prabhat, soon became a leading star of the Hindi cinema and, along with actors Dilip Kumar and Raj Kapoor, dominated the medium for two decades. Since the 1980s, Dev Anand has appeared mainly in his own productions, films that he directs each year with unfailing determination. He admits quite candidly how he hates to think of the past, how he dislikes watching his old movies, and how much more important it is to live in the present. He blends old-world manners and charm with feverish energy — qualities that are evident in his own account of his entry into the Prabhat world:

> I gate-crashed into Mr Baburao Pai's Bombay office; this was in 1946. He said, 'All right, I'll see you,' so I went in. I think he must have been impressed because he said, 'I'll give you a ticket, go to Poona and audition. Go by the Deccan Queen.' I was very happy, he sent me a first-class ticket and I went to Poona. I stayed at Prabhat's guest house and the next day, a director called P.L. Santoshi auditioned me. Then I returned to Bombay and seven days later, I got a telephone call: they liked me, and offered me Rs 350 a month salary, and a contract for three years. In those days, Rs 350 was a lot of money. Out of that money, I used to send Rs 60 to my sister who was studying in Lahore. My first break was in a film on Hindu-Muslim unity, *Hum Ek Hain*. Rehman played the role of the Muslim character and I was the Hindu. People liked the

> film; it did above-average business. It was based on an idea of national unity — a unity that was disrupted.
>
> I met Guru Dutt at Prabhat. We shared a common *dhobi* who gave my clean shirts to Guru Dutt by mistake, and gave me his. Guru Dutt was working with Bedekar, and had a very small role in *Hum Ek Hain*. Guru Dutt, Rehman and I would cycle around the streets of Poona together. We became great pals as we were the same age. Guru Dutt and I promised each other that if he got a chance to direct, then he'd cast me in the leading role, and if I got a chance to produce, then Guru Dutt would direct the picture.

Vasanthi Padukone recounts events of a more personal nature in her memoirs (*Imprint*, 1979) from those Poona days, telling of an early romantic involvement. Guru Dutt had fallen in love with a young dancer, Vijaya, who was also involved with a married man. The man's jealous wife, keen to be rid of Vijaya, tried her best to force Guru Dutt, who was only nineteen at the time, to marry her.

> Somehow the crisis was over. Everything was settled. I thought that it would be better if Guru married to save him from such further calamities. So I chose a Hyderabadi cousin's daughter, Suvarna, for him to marry. He saw the girl and agreed; and Guru and Suvarna wrote to each other. Then suddenly, all correspondence stopped, and the family broke connections with us, and arranged the girl's marriage with another boy.

Mrs. Padukone soon found out that the reason for her cousin's change of mind was a letter that Guru Dutt himself had written to his uncle telling him of the Vijaya incident. Guru Dutt had hoped that his honesty might avert any misunderstanding after the marriage. Guru Dutt's plain-talking did not impress his uncle, who believed, as did many from his social class, that the film world was a disreputable one. Although attitudes have changed over the years, as more and more actors and actresses of all classes have joined the film industry, working in films is still considered — even in the nineties — to be on the borderline of respectability. There are many who firmly believe that people working in films live by moral codes that are different from those of the general population. Love affairs and second marriages are quite commonplace in the film world, and marrying into it was deemed a risky business in those days. Vasanthi Padukone's cousin felt no different. Guru Dutt did not show his feelings to anyone, and no one knew whether he felt any disappointment in not being able to marry Suvarna.

In 1947, Baburao Pai had given up his partnership in Prabhat Film Company, and moved to Bombay where he started his own concern, Famous Pictures and Studios. At Vasanthi Padukone's request, Pai gave Guru Dutt a job at his Bombay studios as assistant to director Anadinath Banerji for the film *Mohan* (1947). Dev Anand, who had by that time also left Prabhat and taken to freelancing, starred in *Mohan*. After having spent two years at Prabhat, Guru Dutt returned to the family home in Matunga.

The financial struggle never seemed to end for the Padukones. Vasanthi had to give private tuition in addition to her job as a school teacher. Atmaram was sent on holiday to Calcutta, but on his return, he had to give up his studies in order to find employment. At the end of 1947, after having completed his contract with Baburao Pai, Guru Dutt found himself out of work for almost a year. The depression and despondency of being aimless made its mark on Guru Dutt. Until that point in time, he had managed to achieve the dreams of his youth; his passion for dance had led him to Almora, his desire to learn film-making had taken him to Prabhat, but now he found real obstacles before him. Guru Dutt became aware of how little an artist is valued in a materialistic world, and how personal talent alone cannot satisfy a creative mind. In those desolate days, soon after Partition, Guru Dutt wrote the first draft of *Pyaasa* which he originally called 'Kashmakash' (Conflict). Money problems, and growing tensions in the family resulting from the difficult relationship between his parents, added to Guru Dutt's desire to succeed, and to his need to be recognized. The mood and tensions of those days found expression in *Pyaasa*; his dispirited view of the world reflects the reality of those trying months. His sister Lalitha remembers how Guru Dutt would submit his short stories to the British editor of *The Illustrated Weekly of India*, C.R. Mandy; the stories always came back accompanied by a rejection note. Atmaram and Guru Dutt were so disillusioned by the lack of opportunities to find work that they contemplated opening a bookshop near King's Circle in Matunga.

After months of struggle, Guru Dutt finally managed to get a job as an assistant to Amiya Chakravarty. Chakravarty was a leading director of the forties, and had worked closely with Devika Rani in the running of the famous Bombay Talkies after the death of the studio's founder Himansu Rai in 1940. By the end of 1943, internal conflict at Bombay Talkies resulted in two rival factions being formed. Devika Rani and Chakravarty found themselves in opposition to Sashadhar Mukherjee and his colleagues (including Gyan Mukherjee, Ashok Kumar and Rai Bahadur Chunilal). As a result, S. Mukherjee, Rai Bahadur Chunilal, Ashok Kumar and Gyan Mukherjee left Bombay Talkies, and, in March 1943, they formed their own company, Filmistan, in the old Sharda Movietone studios in Goregaon (Bombay). By 1949, Amiya Chakravarty had also left Bombay Talkies and was working under an independent banner when he made *Girls School* (released in 1949). While Guru Dutt worked on *Girls School* as an assistant, he began a friendship with the film's leading actress, Geeta Bali.

After *Girls School*, Guru Dutt became an assistant to Gyan Mukherjee on Bombay Talkies' film *Sangram* (1950), a crime thriller starring Ashok Kumar and Nalini Jaywant. Gyan Mukherjee was an important role model for Guru Dutt, who like himself was a kind of outsider to the film world. Mukherjee had studied at Allahabad University, and had worked as a scientist at the Indian Science Institute in Calcutta. His friend Sashadhar Mukherjee had persuaded him to join his team at Bombay Talkies, initially as a writer.

ATMARAM: Guru Dutt left Prabhat in 1947, the year we got our Independence and there was Partition. There was a big set-back in the film industry then, and Guru Dutt was out of a job for almost a year. After that, he joined Gyan Mukherjee who was a very big name in commercial cinema at that time. He had directed *Kismet* [1943] which ran for something like four or five years in one cinema hall. *Kismet* was an all-time hit. Guru Dutt was very close to Gyanji, who was a brilliant man. He was the intellectual mind behind the hits of Bombay Talkies. He had an excellent library, and was an educated person. Bombay Talkies had a story workshop, a group of four or five writers working together; they included P.L. Santoshi, Shahid Lateef, Gyan Mukherjee, and of course, S. Mukherjee himself. Guru Dutt had very great regard for Gyanji, and though Gyanji had a big name, his later films were unsuccessful.

At the time of Partition in 1947, several Muslim technicians and actors migrated to Pakistan. Partition also brought thousands of Hindu refugees to India from East Bengal, Sind and West Punjab. Some of the many thousand refugees joined the expanding and changing Bombay film industry. Films were no longer produced in studios, but independently. The move away from the studio system of production had in fact started in the early forties when financiers who had made their money on the black market during the war years offered large fees — including cash payments — to the leading actors of the time. The prospect of making vast sums was a great temptation and many actors, music directors (who combine the functions of composer-arranger and sometimes conductor) and technicians joined the freelance sector on a contract basis. Another major blow to the studio system was the restriction on the import of film stock during the war years. These restrictions not only meant that studios produced fewer films while still having to pay a large and idle staff. The war years also meant that studios were compelled to make 'war effort' films dealing with themes concerning the current situation. The financial crisis that the studios faced was aggravated by the fact that many of the original founders had either died (for example, Himansu Rai of Bombay Talkies died in 1940) or had chosen to establish their own production companies. By the early fifties, the New Theatres (Calcutta), Prabhat Film Company (Poona) and Bombay Talkies faced liquidation.

Film production in Bombay was largely controlled by Hindi-Urdu speaking Punjabis, and a few Bengali groups in which Guru Dutt seemed to fit quite naturally because of his own Calcutta background. He no longer used his family name, Shivshankar Padukone, and became known as simply Guru Dutt (although all legal documents and agreements carry his full name). Many assumed that he was a Bengali as 'Dutt' is a common Bengali surname.

Despite the fact that Guru Dutt and his contemporaries could not depend on the studio system, the work of directors who had developed their skills in the studio era continued to influence this new generation of directors. Gyan Mukherjee's *Kismet* (1943), produced by Bombay Talkies, was an early example of the lost-and-found theme (a recurrent and popular story line in which children are separated from their parents in childhood only to be reunited again through fate and circumstance years later). *Kismet* also provided the popular model of the anti-hero, a middle-class and usually educated man who turns to crime for survival. Another major influence was Mehboob Khan's *Andaaz* (1949), a love-triangle drama reflecting the dilemmas of the urban rich with their uneasy meeting of eastern and western values in modern India.

Though the conventions of Hindi cinema using the pattern of music and song within its narrative remained largely unaltered from earlier productions, the film of the fifties distinguished itself in many new areas including music. The fact that from the mid-forties play-back singers were systematically recording film songs meant that compositions could be written in a wider musical range. It was also in the late forties and early fifties that many well-established Urdu poets began writing lyrics for the cinema, giving the film song an enhanced poetic legitimacy. The acceptance of play-back singers also encouraged a wider range of actors who were no longer required to have a good singing voice, while the style of performance moved increasingly away from the theatrical to the natural. Innovation in photography and in screenplay-writing that favoured social realism promulgated a kind of renaissance in the popular cinema of Bombay.

By the late forties, Dev Anand had become a fairly well-established actor, having had his first major hit in the 1948 Bombay Talkies' film *Ziddi*, directed by Shahid Lateef. Following the lead of other producers, Dev Anand and his elder brother, Chetan Anand, started their own film production company, Navketan, in 1949. Chetan Anand made his second film, *Afsar*, under the banner of Navketan in 1950. When Uday Shankar's Centre closed down, many of its artists and former students also joined IPTA in Bombay. In 1950, Dev Anand, not forgetting his promise to Guru Dutt who was working as Gyan Mukherjee's assistant at the time, asked him to direct Navketan's second production. Guru Dutt's first film *Baazi* was released on June 15, 1951 at the Swastik cinema in Bombay.

CHAPTER THREE

Baazi

In the August 1951 issue of *Filmindia*, a leading film magazine edited by Baburao Patel (who was a film-maker and publicist before he became an extremely influential film journalist), appeared a very mixed review of Guru Dutt's first film:

> *Baazi* has quite a few beautiful bits in songs and dances, several excellent passages in the dialogue and a beautiful performance by that inimitable artiste Geeta Bali. And if you can forget the unholy mess the director and those two new girls [Roopa Varman and Kalpana Kartik] make, *Baazi* may be seen for its beautiful bits.

Baazi (The Gamble), released in 1951, is the story of Madan (Dev Anand), an unemployed taxi-driver and occasional gambler, who looks after his ailing sister, Roopa (Roopa Varman). Pedro (Rashid Khan), impressed by Madan's luck at cards, urges him to visit the Star Club, a sleazy joint run by con men and gangsters. When Madan ventures to the club, cabaret dancer Nina (Geeta Bali) takes an instant fancy to him and does not delay in telling him so. Madan is not interested in Nina, and instead falls in love with a doctor, Rajani (newcomer Kalpana Kartik, whom Dev Anand married in 1954), whom he meets at a local dispensary. When Madan discovers that his sister has tuberculosis, and wants desperately to pay for her treatment at a sanatorium, he has no choice but to join the con men at the Star Club. The club's ruthless boss (K.N. Singh) turns out to be Rajani's father, and when he is recognized by Madan, he plans to have Madan killed. Nina tries to warn Madan that his life is in danger and in the process she is herself killed, and Madan is framed for the crime. Madan confesses to the murder, fearing that his sister might be harmed, and is tried and sentenced to hang. Rajani's childhood friend, police-officer Ramesh (Dhawan), comes to Madan's rescue and tricks Rajani's father into admitting his guilt. The villain is arrested, and Madan is sentenced for a short term in prison for gambling and cheating. He is then released, and finds Rajani waiting outside the jail for him.

Baazi's screenplay does not rise above the formulaic. The plot is mostly predictable, and the tone of the film follows the conventions of the lightweight thriller. The best moments are the picturizations of the songs, whose sophistication anticipates the subtlety of the style that Guru Dutt was later to develop so skilfully. Guru Dutt lifts scenes from the routine to the unusual, one such example being when Madan visits the Star Club for the first time. As Madan enters the club a cabaret commences, and he finds himself caught in the dancer's net as she draws him into her musical routine to the words of the song *Sharmaaye kahe, ghabraaye kahe* (Why feel shy, why be upset?). This literal ensnaring not only tells of the dancer Nina's desires, but is symbolic of the tangled web of crime in which Madan will eventually be caught. Very much in the Hollywood *film noir* mould, the next sequence has Madan being led through a long corridor in which one door opens to reveal yet another. Finally after passing through a sequence of mysteriously-opening doors, Madan is in the gang-leader's den.

The climax of the song *Suno gajar kya gaaye* (Heed the cry of the bird) is a remarkable example of Guru Dutt's use of close-ups and rhythm in editing. Nina has learnt of the plot to kill Madan. She tries to warn him but cannot as she is being watched. Night falls, and it is time for Nina to perform her cabaret routine. Madan is seated at a table among the guests, and the killers stand near the bar. Nina tries to warn Madan of the imminent danger to his life through the words of her song. Guru Dutt builds and maintains the tension brilliantly between the different centres of action involving Nina and the dancers, the unsuspecting Madan, and the killers waiting for their moment to strike. The climax of the song is divided into fourteen shots cut between a continually moving crane shot (from high to low level) of Nina and the dancers and a series of close-ups of eyes. We see a shot of Nina, cut to a close-up of a revolver being pulled out of a jacket, back to Nina, cut to a close-up of the killer's eyes, back to Nina, cut to a close-up of Madan's eyes, etc. We expect the sound of gunfire to punctuate the song's last musical phrase, but Madan is not shot; instead the sound of applause announces the end of the scene.

Play-back singer Geeta Roy's rendition of *Tadbeer se bigdi hui taqdeer bana le* (Find a way to right your damaged fate) performed by actress Geeta Bali is another fine example of Guru Dutt's natural instinct for using songs that not only hold attention for their own poetic and artistic merit but also advance the story. The words of the song, continuing 'Believe in yourself and throw the dice' acts as a catalyst for Madan. The struggle with his conscience is over, and by the end of the scene, Madan has decided to throw the dice, gamble with his life and join the Star Club.

Like Raju in Raj Kapoor's *Awaara* (released in the same year as *Baazi*), Madan is very much a fifties screen hero, a loner unprotected by class or family, who is willing to bend moral codes in order to survive. In *Baazi,* criminality is seen to be an easy route to social mobility. When Madan, a taxi-driver, becomes a con man and wears fancy clothes, he boasts of attracting college girls. The implication is that he has become acceptable to all classes. The old view of right and wrong becomes blurred as Madan's values are determined by an instinct for survival rather than by a belief in traditional norms. The popularity of Madan's role in *Baazi* was said to inspire Chetan Anand to create a film around the same character titled *Taxi Driver* (1954), also starring Dev Anand. The heroine in *Baazi* is seen as being blind to social differences, and believes that even criminals can be reformed through love. Audiences seemed to identify with the new heroes of popular cinema, as they themselves were in the process of social transformation.

An intriguing feature of the film is Guru Dutt's own brief appearance. *Baazi*'s first shot is a low-angle view of a doorway where a barely noticeable, and unidentified man sits observing the street. As a car enters the frame, the young man (Guru Dutt) seated at the threshold turns to look towards the camera for a fleeting moment, then looks away again. Pedro (actor Rashid Khan) steps out of the car and walks through the doorway followed by the gaze of the young man, who is clearly down on his luck. It is not unusual for directors to appear in their films, the most famous example of course being that of Alfred Hitchcock. Hitchcock's screen appearances are almost a distracting feature of his work, because it is only when he has appeared, preferably early in the film, that audiences stop looking out for him and allow themselves to become involved in the story. Most often these personal winks to an informed audience are based on the premise that the director has star status. Guru Dutt, who was unknown to audiences at this stage of his career, appears not as a forgettable passer-by, but precisely as the screen character that he developed in his later films: the young man at the doorway could easily be Vijay of *Pyaasa*, or Suresh Sinha of *Kaagaz ke Phool*, withdrawn and defeated.

Guru Dutt does return in later films to settings and characterizations similar to those seen in *Baazi*. Conversations in a moving car between the hero and the heroine, or driver and passenger, occur again in *Aar Paar* and *Mr & Mrs 55*. The car or taxi is an ideal setting to lightly suggest social differences; the hero is the employed driver, and the passenger the more privileged, and the occasion of travel (as so often in Indian narratives) supplies a natural context for people of distinct social backgrounds to be thrown together. Sung somewhat in the style of the forties' songs, *Baazi*'s comic song *Dil ye kya cheez hai* (What is this thing, a heart?) performed by Kishore Kumar for Dev Anand involves the participation of ordinary people who happen to pass by on the road — a familiar feature in Guru Dutt's later comedies. Madan and Kalu (of *Aar Paar*) are also similar in their behaviour, both displaying an equal measure of coyness and cockiness: the otherwise brazen heroes run for cover to avoid being seen emerging half-dressed from a bath when their loved ones appear.

VIJAY PADUKONE: In 1950, the five of us, Guru Dutt, Atma, Lalli, Devi and I, along with other children from the neighbourhood in Matunga hopped on a tram — those days we had trams in Bombay — we were celebrating our Republic Day [January 26] and the entire city was decorated. I was about 9 years old at the time.

Guru Dutt would ask me to buy him his cigarettes — Gold Flake. Those were the days when he was signed by Dev Anand for *Baazi*. Guru Dutt would go by bus to the Famous Cine in Mahalaxmi where Dev Anand had his offices. During the making of the film, Dev Sahib's van used to come every morning to pick up Guru Dutt. The shooting used to take place at Famous. I must have been 10 years old when I went to the sets to see a night shooting. They were filming a serious scene between Geeta Bali and Dev Anand. During a break, Geeta gave me a coke to drink. When the next shot was ready and the dialogue was being filmed, I burped loudly. Guru Dutt lost his cool, he came over to me and fired me. He said, 'Take this boy back home.' Geeta came to my rescue. That was the first time I saw him on the sets.

As well as bringing the excitement of making a first film, *Baazi* allowed Guru Dutt to work with many talented people. Although the celebrated Urdu poet Sahir Ludhianvi had already written for the film *Naujawan* in 1950, it was the success of *Baazi*'s songs that helped establish his name as a film lyricist. Music director S.D. Burman's score was also greatly appreciated and in particular, the song *Tadbeer se bigdi hui taqdeer bana le* created a tremendous stir — audiences were said to return again and again to the cinema hall just for this one song. Cinema Vision's special 1983 issue, *The Golden Age of Hindi Film Music*, edited by Siddharth Kak, includes an article by S.D.Burman titled, 'Far away from the world of music,' in which Burman comments:

> The most important experiment in this film was a *ghazal* — *Tadbeer se bigdi hui taqdeer bana le* — set to music in the Western style and sung by play-back singer Geeta Roy. When the film was ready for release I too got anxious. Had I made a mistake? When I went to Calcutta for a holiday, the records of *Baazi* had come into the market. After a few days, one of my friends suggested we go fishing in Itchhapore. Football and fishing have always been my two great loves... We did not catch any fish. In fact, a gang of urchins was busy frolicking in the water and the fish had decided to stay at the bottom. I wanted to shoo the urchins out of the water. But as I approached them, I heard them singing. I forgot about fishing because the experiment had worked: *Tadbeer se bigdi hui* ... was the song they were singing.

Guru Dutt shared *Baazi*'s story credit with Balraj Sahni, who until 1949 was a key figure in IPTA. Through the work of its many talented members, IPTA had an indirect but powerful influence on Hindi cinema, bringing to it a genuine sense of social concern. Sahni started acting in films in 1946 in Abbas's *Dharti ke Lal*, and occasionally provided the Hindi dubbing for Russian films. The dubbing took place at the Famous Studios building in Mahalaxmi where Chetan and Dev Anand had opened their Navketan offices. Chetan Anand, who had studied with Balraj Sahni at the Government College in Lahore, and was a fellow IPTA member, invited Sahni to work on *Baazi*. In his autobiography, *Balraj Sahni by Balraj Sahni* (Hind Pocket Books, Delhi 1979), Sahni makes reference to the experience of working with Guru Dutt. Sahni had felt that Guru Dutt's script was too weak, and wanted more time to work on the scenes and dialogues. Sahni remembers the many all-night sessions that they had in Sahni's home, and in Guru Dutt's flat at Matunga. While Sahni believed that the most important element in a film was the screenplay, he felt that Guru Dutt — influenced by Sashadhar Mukherjee's school of filmmaking — gave more importance to the songs. Mukherjee allegedly believed that a screenplay should be 'artificial and rickety', making the viewers impatient for a song; Mukherjee thought that if the viewers were too engrossed in the story, they would regard the song or the dance as an unwanted intrusion. Sahni describes the difficulty they had in finding the ending of the film, and how he and Guru Dutt had gone for advice to director/writer Zia Sarhadi. Sarhadi resolved the problem by borrowing the idea of *Baazi*'s ending from an old Hollywood film.

Baazi and *Hulchul* (1951) — the film that Sahni was acting in at the time — were on the sets simultaneously and, consequently, Sahni never visited *Baazi*'s sets. He only became aware of the film's progress through the reports given to him by Guru Dutt's assistants, Raj Khosla and Kuldeep Kohli. When Sahni learnt that the screenplay had undergone many changes, including the inclusion of three additional songs, Sahni complained to Chetan Anand. These differences created a coldness in Sahni's relationship with Guru Dutt and they did not work together again.

The effects of *Baazi*'s success on Guru Dutt's life were multiple and included an excited Guru Dutt buying the first ceiling-fan for the family flat in Matunga. He was twenty-six years old and in love with the playback singer, Geeta Roy, whom he had met at the recording of *Tadbeer se bigdi hui*. Geeta Roy was born in Faridpur (now in Bangladesh) and as a child she had trained under music teacher, Hirendranath Nandy. In 1942, during the Quit India movement, her family left East Bengal to settle in Bombay. Like Guru Dutt's own parents, the Roys had little money, and could no longer afford to pay for Geeta's singing lessons. Though composer Hanuman Prasad introduced her in *Bhakta Prahlad* in 1946, it was through music director S.D. Burman that Geeta Roy had her first major hit in the song *Mera sundar sapna beet gaya* (My beautiful dream is over). The song was recorded for the film *Do Bhai* (1947), and despite the apprehension of its producer, S.D. Burman insisted that Geeta sing the song. Geeta was only fifteen at the time, but the mesmerizing effect of her voice was immediate, and the song was followed by a number of similar successes. Geeta Roy worked with nearly all the leading music directors of her time, and already had star status when Guru Dutt and his family first met her during the *mahurat* (auspicious date and time for the commencement of shooting) of *Baazi*. The first scene that was filmed on that day happened to be Geeta Roy's song *Tadbeer se bigdi hui* picturized on actress Geeta Bali.

Soon Geeta Roy began visiting Guru Dutt in Matunga, and despite her success and fame, she showed a humility which endeared her to the whole Padukone family. Vasanthi Padukone remembers how Geeta would sing a favourite Bengali song *Tumi jodi bolo bhalobasha*, much to the delight of Guru Dutt who was very much in love. Though the young couple were anxious to marry, Geeta's family was reluctant to lose the breadwinner of the household, and the wedding was postponed for two years.

ATMARAM: *Baazi* was a big success. It ran for 25 weeks in one cinema. And it established Guru Dutt as a director. Geeta was one of the top singers at that time and that's how they met, during the making of the film, and then later married. Geeta had a very vivacious personality; she was a very great singer and a wonderful person. They had two sons, Tarun (born in 1954), Arun (born in 1956) and a daughter, Nina (born in 1962). Geeta contributed a lot to the success of Guru Dutt's films in the early years.

Baazi was the start of many things in Guru Dutt's life and career, including his association with comedian Johnny Walker. By the mid-fifties, Johnny Walker had become a leading comedian of the Hindi cinema, and many films were sold at the box-office on his name alone. Johnny Walker was born Badruddin Jamaluddin Kazi in Indore; his family settled in Bombay when he was in his teens. Badruddin had little money, and worked briefly as a conductor on Bombay's BEST buses before becoming an extra in films. Badruddin first made a mark by playing a drunkard or a street hawker to entertain the actors of *Hulchul* — in which he was an extra — during their lunch break. Balraj Sahni was so impressed by Badruddin's natural talent that he promised to find him work when he could, and that opportunity came in *Baazi*. Sahni instructed Badruddin to barge into the Navketan's offices where Chetan Anand, Dev Anand, Guru Dutt and Sahni were working. Badruddin's routine as a drunkard greatly amused everyone present, and when Balraj Sahni told Badruddin to take a bow, the switch in personality from the ranting drunkard to the soberest of men deeply impressed his audience. Despite the fact that *Baazi* was nearly half-completed, Guru Dutt devised a role for him in the film.

JOHNNY WALKER: There is a scene in *Baazi* in which Madan [Dev Anand] is given a letter in prison by a drunk. I played that part. Guru Dutt said, 'There isn't much dialogue in the scene. Take this letter and go into the cell. Say whatever crosses your mind, just like you did when you entered my office.' I thought to myself, 'Here's my chance', so I laid it on thick, I was pretty good at that. *Baazi* was the first film in which people noticed me. Before that whenever I'd take a friend to the cinema to see a film in which I had acted, I'd appear and then disappear before we knew what happened. *Baazi* was my first film, and it was Guru Dutt's first film. I have worked in almost every film he made. God has been kind to me.

Though he is credited under his real name in *Baazi* and in *Jaal*, Badruddin's impersonations of a drunkard seemed a natural enough reason for the comedian to take on the screen name of a whisky brand from *Baaz* onwards. Like Johnny Walker, Raj Khosla, who became a leading director and producer in his own right, also began his film career in *Baazi*. Khosla had dreamt of becoming a play-back singer, but his friend Dev Anand suggested that until he made a name in singing he could work at Navketan. Raj Khosla worked as Guru Dutt's assistant in four films: *Baazi*, *Baaz*, *Jaal* and *Aar Paar*. Though uncredited, Raj Khosla appears in a small role in *Baazi* as a police superintendent who believes that Madan is guilty of Nina's murder. Despite Raj Khosla's genuine love for his friend and mentor, he never believed that he really understood Guru Dutt. Raj Khosla's sad and happy memories of him have always moved him, sometimes to tears:

> In those days, I was trying to be a play-back singer. I knew Dev Anand and one day he told me, 'Raj, there's a friend of mine called Guru Dutt.' I remember that sentence, you know, 'a friend of mine called Guru Dutt.' Dev mentioned his name casually — and to imagine that one day that name would be world famous!
>
> Dev said to me, 'Guru Dutt is going to direct my next picture. Why don't you become his assistant? Come on, Raj, we'll work together, soon you'll be able to sing too.' So I met Guru Dutt and he asked me, 'Have you any experience in assisting?'. I said, 'Yes, I have.' Tommy-rot, I knew nothing about film-making. The second thing he asked, 'Do you know Hindi?'. I replied, 'Of course I know Hindi.' I couldn't actually write in Hindi. I'm from Punjab, Gurdaspur, so I knew Urdu. In those days, in the Punjab learning Urdu was very common; even now you will find that many Punjabis who are over forty know how to write Urdu, not Hindi. Guru Dutt said, 'Okay, start from tomorrow.' I ran from there and the first thing I got was an Hindi alphabet book. I started learning the alphabet: *'ka kha...'* Sure enough, after about six or seven days, Guru Dutt said, 'Copy out these dialogue scenes.' By that time I had picked up some Hindi. As I was writing a scene he asked, 'When did you start learning Hindi?'. I said, 'On the day you asked me if I knew the language.' He said, 'Fine, it doesn't matter. Give this to Kuldeep [Guru Dutt's second assistant on *Baazi*], let him write them out.' We liked each other instantaneously.

Despite the success of *Baazi*, rumours abounded of tension between producer Chetan Anand and Guru Dutt. Chetan Anand was said to believe that Guru Dutt could not direct actress Kalpana Kartik competently, so he took over the filming himself for three shooting days. Guru Dutt considered resigning, but his friend Dev Anand intervened and made sure that Guru Dutt was left alone. Working again for Navketan after *Baazi* seemed improbable, and Guru Dutt found a new producer — T.R. Fatehchand of Filmarts, a refugee from Sind — to back his second feature, *Jaal* (The Net). The film was released at the Kamal theatre in Bombay on September 12, 1952.

CHAPTER FOUR

Jaal

The *Filmfare* review of Guru Dutt's second film, *Jaal*, included praise for his authentic portrayal of the Christian fishing community and added, 'Slick direction, competent narration, naive quality about narration... Guru Dutt has done, on the whole, a fairly good job in wielding the megaphone.' The review featured in the November 1952 issue of *Filmindia*, and written by Baburao Patel, reluctantly suggests Guru Dutt's potential:

> For this picture establishes him as a director who knows much of his job and is no longer the amateur of *Baazi*. Guru Dutt entertains in *Jaal* with his smooth direction, and in future if he only adds more purpose and some power to his presentation he could be included among our intelligent directors.

The paragraphs that follow then concentrate on the failures of the director and the film. *Jaal*'s story, written by Guru Dutt, is set in a small village under foreign rule along the West Coast (intended to be Portuguese Goa) where a community of Christian fisherfolk live. Away from the usual screen stereotypes of happy-go-lucky, heavy-drinking Christians, the fishermen are seen as hard-working and honourable. The peaceful life of the community is soon disrupted by the arrival of a Bombay gold smuggler, Tony (Dev Anand). The beautiful fisherwoman, Maria (Geeta Bali), does not heed the advice of her blind brother Carlo (K.N. Singh), her friend Simon (Ramsingh) and Tony's partner in crime, Lisa (Purnima), who together warn her to keep away from the treacherous Tony. Maria soon falls prey to his charms, and while she believes that Tony's love is genuine, he is busy plotting further criminal escapades. The final scene has Maria literally caught in the middle of gunfire between the police and Tony who is on the run. Oblivious of danger, Maria rushes to his side. Though Tony threatens to shoot her, he finds himself incapable of harming her. Maria convinces Tony that no one is completely evil and that he, too, can change. Purified by Maria's love, Tony surrenders to the police knowing that she will wait for him.

Geeta Bali's performance as the God-fearing Maria is remarkably convincing. Maria takes refuge in the teachings of the Church, and believes — as the priest stresses — that those who err must be forgiven. This faith in the power of redemption motivates her to try to change Tony. She never fails to believe that God, and the love she feels for Tony, will save him. The subtext of the film juxtaposes good (the pure world of the rural seaside community) and evil (the corrupt city as seen through the person of Tony). At the altar of a church, Maria makes Tony promise never to deceive her. His promise is soon forgotten as he happily abandons her in the middle of the ocean. Yet she never turns away from him, forgiving his every action. The importance of forgiving those who have strayed from the righteous path is highlighted at the opening of the film by an on-screen text which also forms part of the local priest's Sunday sermon:

> Heed not the speaker of evil,
> Judge not the evil-doer,
> Stop those who stray from the path
> Forgive those who have sinned

Jaal is the only Guru Dutt film whose protagonists are guided by religious forces. His personal interest in religion was not confined to his own background and origins (as a Saraswat he himself was a Brahmin), but encompassed a curiosity about the teachings of other religions, including Islam and Christianity. In his films, Guru Dutt always showed a secular India in which his screen characters, all belonging to different castes and creeds, interact freely. Though *Jaal* is primarily set in a Christian milieu, religious activity is not limited to church scenes, and the many sounds of the fishing village include the Muslim call to prayer.

In an interview in *Screen* published in April 1952, and reprinted by film historian Firoze Rangoonwalla in his book *Guru Dutt, 1925-1965: a Monograph* (published in 1973 by the National Film Archives of India, Poona), Guru Dutt comments:

> One of the chief aims of a director should be to select subjects with inherent human values and illustrate them cleverly with incidents... For my part, I would prefer the golden mean of

handling a simple subject packed with illustrations. My picture, *Jaal*, is on these lines and it is considered a success.

While earlier films based on the figure of the anti-hero, such as Gyan Mukherjee's 1943 production, *Kismet*, had triumphed, there was no guarantee that audiences would identify with the unscrupulous Tony. The flaws of *Jaal* are found principally in the uneven development of its characters, and in the film's unfulfilled ambition of being a crime thriller. Scenes involving Tony's plans to smuggle gold with his side-kick (played by Badruddin who had not as yet adopted the screen name Johnny Walker), and Arab accomplices (played by assistant Raj Khosla and dialogue writer, M.A. Lateef) are treated so comically that it seems hard to accept Tony as a dangerous gangster. *Jaal*'s many ponderous scenes involving Maria, her brother Carlo (K.N. Singh), and the farcical police officer Gomez (Rashid Khan) do little to maintain dramatic tension.

Though Guru Dutt did not manage to make *Jaal* work as a thriller, he did achieve success in his picturization of its songs, and in the way that he gave otherwise ordinary scenes a specially visual feel. One such example is the scene in which Tony, Lisa and Maria go to the village fair. Lisa insists that Maria take a ride with her on the ferris wheel. Tony stands at the foot of the wheel looking up as Lisa and Maria are carried high into the air. Lisa takes advantage of their being alone, and tells Maria that Tony is the ruthless man who has ruined her life. With each turn of the wheel Maria's view of Tony is being altered, physically and psychologically. The impact of Lisa's warning has Maria's world turning upside-down.

The song sequences in the film work particularly well in themselves, but are also helped by the fact that Guru Dutt makes sure to set up a song in the scene that precedes it, and ensures that its impact continues to be felt in the scene that follows. Tony tells Maria that when he calls, she will come to him. She adamantly denies all feelings for him as he repeats that she will come to him that very night. As night falls and the moon is high in the sky, Tony's seductive song, *Ye raat ye chaandni phir kahaan, sun ja dil ki dastaan* (This night and this moonlight may never return, hear the story of my heart) is carried by a gust of wind that forces open the doors to Maria's room. She comes out onto the balcony and hears his song. Trying to escape the power of its words, Maria closes the door and re-enters her room. No longer able to resist the enticement of the present (*Raat ye bahaar ki phir kabhi na aayegi* — This night of spring may never return), she is drawn out of her house in an almost trance-like state. The song ends with a dramatic crane shot (from low to high angle) that matches the music as it ascends to its climax. Love has triumphed and Maria rushes to Tony's side. They embrace for a long moment without speaking. As she makes her way out onto the beach she is caught in a fishing net — a reference to the 'net' of the film's title and a symbol of the snares of love.

Each of Guru Dutt's brothers and his cousin Shyam Benegal, joined films as producers and directors. Shyam Benegal's powerful first film *Ankur* (1974) was an early example of the New Wave in Indian cinema, a movement which attracted much international interest and recognition. When Shyam Benegal was around sixteen, he had visited Guru Dutt briefly on the sets of *Baazi*, but was not influenced by his elder cousin's style of filmmaking when he came to make his own films. The most obvious way in which directors of the New Wave showed their difference was their deliberate exclusion of songs. Guru Dutt himself had always wanted to see Hindi films without songs to appeal to audiences, and had even asked Waheeda Rehman to pray for the success of B.R. Chopra's *Kanoon* (1960), an early attempt at a songless film. Though Guru Dutt might have wanted to break away from this important convention of Hindi cinema, Shyam Benegal believes that the way Guru Dutt filmed songs was one of his greatest talents:

> In terms of film technique what he has left behind is the way he picturized songs. It was his contribution to Indian cinema, and it has had a tremendous impact on anybody who has made films after him. He was very much part of the tradition of Indian cinema, but he had a young man's romantic vision: most Indian film-makers have a romantic vision, but in his case, it was combined with a choice of things of literary value. He had a fine sensibility and I think he had considerable taste — that was evident from the very first film that he made.
>
> My first memory of him was when he came to our home in Hyderabad. During the summer vacations most of our cousins used to come and spend their holidays with us. In those days, Guru Dutt was with Uday Shankar in Almora. He stayed with us for a week. I remember very vividly that he had this long, flowing hair and did a snake-charmer dance on the terrace of our house one evening. He has been a great inspiration simply because he succeeded; he was young and he went ahead and did things which at that time seemed impossible. This is what later strengthened my resolve to come into the movies and make films myself.

Viewers and critics alike have shared Shyam Benegal's appreciation of Guru Dutt's skill in song picturization. One fine example amongst many is the way he introduces the female version of the song, *Ye raat ye chaandni phir kahaan*. Maria has reluctantly been persuaded to forget Tony and marry another. After her engagement ceremony is performed, she walks out alone on the beach. In the harshness of daylight, Maria imagines hearing in the distance the song once sung to her by the now-estranged Tony. The song *Ye raat ye chaandni phir kahaan* echoing in the distance is used as a musical flashback evoking the fateful night of their union. Maria's song is her reply: *Chaandni raaten pyaar ki baaten kho gayiin jaane kahaan* (Where have those moonlit nights, those words of love now fled?).

DEV ANAND: I remember a funny incident when we were shooting the sequence for the song *Ye raat ye chaandni phir kahaan*. A friend of mine came to see me on the set. He took me to a small cottage while Guru Dutt was taking a shot of Geeta Bali. My friend gave me a glass of *feni* [a Goan drink similar to vodka]; I liked it and took another glass, and another. When I returned for the shot, I was doing all sorts of antics. I got hold of Geeta and walked straight into the sea. I had a lovely watch which got totally damaged and all I remember was that we had to pack up. We were all very wet, and I was laughing away. I had a tremendous hangover the next day.

Despite the evident shortcomings of the film, the choice of outdoor locations (*Jaal* was filmed near Ratnagiri on the coast between Bombay and Goa) is a relief from the usual studio sets predominant in Hindi cinema. Boats at sea, village fairs, Sunday church services, fisherfolk at work, all contribute to the creation of an authentic world. As in *Baazi*, Guru Dutt appears briefly in *Jaal*, this time as a fisherman, involved in the collective work of bringing in the day's catch. He is seen unshaven, shirtless and wearing a cap as he joins in the chorus of Maria's song that urges the fisherfolk to pull in their heavy nets, *Zor lagaake pair jamaake jaan laraake, haiya!* (Pull with all your might, friends, pull for all you're worth!).

ATMARAM: I was not assisting Guru Dutt in *Baazi*, but I started working with him in *Jaal* in 1952. *Jaal* was based to a large extent on *Bitter Rice* [Giuseppe De Santis's 1948 Italian film *Riso Amaro*]. He was a very hard task-master, disciplined and very much dedicated to his work. On the sets it was difficult to say what exactly was in his mind. He tended to keep everything to himself and wouldn't communicate with the assistants, which made things rather difficult. So he shouted a lot. He often used to set the shot by making his artists stand in a particular frame and look through the view-finder and develop the idea of the shot through the view-finder. Often I would stand in for some other artists and there would be a lot of shouting. Looking back on his films, one realizes what a fine visual sense he had. Films have so many facets but the most important is that it is a visual medium and there lies Guru Dutt's strength: he was able to communicate to the audience visually first — in a brilliant way.

Guru Dutt was always said to be a man of few words, though he clearly had an instinct for choosing talented people to work with him. This instinct served him well from the very start of his career. When viewing the rushes of *Baazi*, he immediately recognized the potential of the film's camera assistant, V.K. Murthy.

V.K. MURTHY: A month before *Baazi* was made, Guru Dutt used to visit the sets of *Afsar* [1950, Navketan's first production] with Raj Khosla to talk to Chetan Anand. I would wonder who was this young, handsome man. Later on, I asked Dev Anand. Dev said, 'His name is Guru Dutt. We were at Prabhat together and he's going to direct a film for us.' In those days, technicians were employed by the studio who supplied the camera equipment to the producer. I was working at Famous Studios, Mahalaxmi, and had to assist whichever cameraman came there to shoot. Navketan's *Baazi* was being produced at Famous; and I was an assistant to the cameraman, V. Ratra.

There was a difficult shot in *Baazi*, so I made a suggestion and Guru Dutt liked it very much. The shot is in the song *Suno gajar kya gaaye*. Dev Anand is standing at a bar with his back to the dance floor. There is a huge mirror above the bar. I started the shot in close-up through the mirror, then panned down to Dev Anand, who starts moving towards the dais where the dance is being performed. I follow him and compose the dancers, and Dev Anand goes and sits on a chair in the foreground. It was not just a panning shot, but a tracking and trolley movement; from top to lower level and a forward movement. In those days, the cameras were huge and the cameraman couldn't take the shot, the reason being that he was a little fat. I shot three takes. One of them was perfect. One day, after we packed up, Guru Dutt said, 'Murthy, from next picture onwards you will be my cameraman.'

V.K. Murthy was born in Mysore in 1923 and even before he had passed his matriculation exam, he was certain that he wanted to work in films. In 1941, following a few failed attempts to find work in the studios of Bombay, Murthy returned home to Madras. His passion for music led him to learning the violin. During the Quit India movement, young Murthy found himself in prison for five months. This brief period as a freedom fighter was followed by a six-month contract as a violinist in dancer Ram Gopal's troupe. In 1946, Murthy completed a course in cinematography at the Polytechnic Institute in Madras and went to Bombay to seek training. Like many young technicians, Murthy found it difficult to get a job in a camera unit, so he played the violin for a few film songs in order to earn his living. After much struggle, Murthy finally became assistant to Fali Mistry, a cinematographer whom he deeply admired. He followed Mistry when he left Lakshmi Studios to join Famous Cine Studios and Laboratories. After working on *Baazi* as an assistant, V.K. Murthy photographed all of Guru Dutt's films (save *Chaudhvin ka Chand*) starting with *Jaal*. Murthy is a quiet and modest man who never boasts of his tremendous contribution to Guru Dutt's work. His smiling eyes light up when he speaks of his favourite director:

> *Jaal* was the beginning of his career. He definitely became more and more confident. When he conceived the story of *Jaal*, we sat together and he narrated it to me for about a week. Then I didn't see him for two or three days. When we met again, he said, 'Murthy, I have another story.' And he narrated the story of *Pyaasa*. I persuaded him not to do *Pyaasa*, and said, 'People have accepted you now. *Baazi* has a background of crime and action. Gain some more popularity, make two or three more films like *Baazi* and once people have accepted you as a big director, you can change, then make *Pyaasa*.'

Another important member of the team was S. Guruswamy, who joined Guru Dutt during the making of *Jaal*, and remained in charge of production until Guru Dutt's last film. Guruswamy had previously worked at Bombay Talkies from 1938, where his uncle, Mr Iyer, headed the accounts department. Following Himansu Rai's death in 1940, Guruswamy became Devika Rani's private secretary, also working at Bombay Talkies as a production secretary until 1947. Guruswamy is a gentle man whose own life is entwined with an important period in the history of Indian cinema. He is a discreet person, matter-of-fact in his understanding of people. Though he is reluctant to make his long association with Guru Dutt very public, his attachment to Guru Dutt is undiminished by time:

I was very fortunate to work with two very good artists: Devika Rani, and an equally good artist of the younger generation, Guru Dutt. He had a good heart and a good understanding. We used to think in unison. He treated me more like a family member, and he'd talk to me freely.

We were all staying in Matunga during the shooting of *Jaal*. I was looking after all the production. For the shooting of the film, we went to Malwan — it's on the coast, just before Ratnagiri. It's a beautiful place. One day we went out to sea to fix up the camera for the next day's shooting. Murthy and I used to be together all the time. The fellow who was supposed to take us out to sea, and bring us back, disappeared. So we went out on our own. The whole night we slogged. The carpenter who was with us would not stop vomiting because he was sea-sick, so Murthy had to go down on his knees and do all the carpentry work. The next morning at five o'clock the fellow reappears. He got a good firing. Another time, Guru Dutt, Murthy and I went out to sea to film, and suddenly the boat's engine failed. I could tell that Guru Dutt was damned worried, but he didn't show it. Somehow we got back.

Baazi and *Jaal* share similar moments, such as an identical frame composition involving Geeta Bali and Dev Anand who are seated at a table in a night-club. In *Baazi*, the couple are chatting at a table and turn back to watch the villain (K.N. Singh) sitting himself down at an adjoining table at the night-club; in *Jaal*, Geeta Bali and Dev Anand are composed in the same way, seated at a table in a night-club, when they turn back to look at the dancer-singer whose song *Door kahin ek taara karta hai ye ishaara* (From afar a star sends you this sign) warns Maria of Tony's treachery. The similarity in feel in Guru Dutt's first films may in part be due to the fact that *Jaal* has the same cast, the same music director and the same lyricist as *Baazi*. Guru Dutt's tendency to work with the same team and to re-cast the same actors was an early pattern. When Guru Dutt planned to make *Jaal* with another producer and not Navketan, he still asked Raj Khosla to continue working with him as assistant. Chetan Anand told Raj Khosla to decide whether he would stay on at Navketan or go with Guru Dutt.

RAJ KHOSLA: Destiny was kind to me: I opted for Guru Dutt. I worked as his assistant in *Jaal*. He wanted me to sing for *Jaal*, the song *Ye raat ye chaandni;* he even recorded me but I failed the test. S.D. Burman said, 'Guru, not now. He's too raw, he can't make it.' Guru Dutt was very upset as he had wanted me to sing that song.

I remember that Guru Dutt had *Pyaasa* in his mind right from the start. At that time he called it 'Kashmakash.' That script was in his heart. I found that Guru Dutt was searching for himself; I found him vacillating in those days, especially in *Jaal*, which didn't have a complete script. *Baazi* had a complete script written by Balraj Sahni. Guru Dutt was bogged down with the *Jaal* script; but he was very conscious that there was something wrong with it. He would often tell me, 'Raj, something is wrong with me. I am not able to catch hold of things, I can't grasp it.' Dev Anand was his star in *Baazi* and in *Jaal*. Dev had his own style, and Guru Dutt couldn't bring him to do what he wanted, so he used to get irritated. And they were very dear friends, so he couldn't push Dev too far either, and Dev would not change; he is still the same, he'll still hold his pose and sing with his own exuberance. So Guru Dutt decided he would become an actor — only for one reason — to portray the character of the hero as it should be. Guru Dutt was not a good actor to begin with. He was very awkward and self-conscious in *Baaz*, but he had an iron will. Any other man would have been broken after the failure of *Baaz*. The film flopped. Any other man would have just broken down, abandoned acting and gone back to direction, but he stuck it out.

CHAPTER FIVE

Baaz

In April 1952, Guru Dutt moved to a flat in an apartment block called Sunder Villa on 12th Road in the Bombay suburb of Khar with his mother, sister Lalitha, and brothers Devi and Vijay. Shivshankar Padukone and Atmaram stayed on in the Matunga flat. Vasanthi Padukone remembers the peace and calm of the green fields surrounding the Khar apartment, and the golden retriever called Tony (after *Jaal*'s hero) which Guru Dutt gave her. Their neighbour, actress Kuldeep Kaur, became a frequent visitor. Meanwhile, Guru Dutt finally managed to persuade Geeta Roy's family to consent to their long-postponed engagement, and a ceremony was held at Matunga's Poddar College.

Later in the same year, on September 5, 1952, Guru Dutt started a production company in partnership with Haridarshan Kaur, Geeta Bali's elder sister. The company was called H.G. Films, after the initials of its two partners. The first film they planned to produce had a Portuguese background and was a costume drama called *Baaz* (The Falcon). Guru Dutt could not cast Dev Anand in the role of *Baaz*'s hero since Dev Anand had become so popular by the early fifties that his fees were unaffordable. Guru Dutt considered actors Shekhar and Sajjan for the film, but at the last moment he changed his mind and decided to play the part of Prince Ravi himself. *Baaz* was the first film in which Guru Dutt appeared in the lead role; but as Guruswamy points out, it failed to convince as a high-seas adventure film:

> Geeta Bali's sister told Guru Dutt, 'Why don't you try acting?' He never believed he could act, he had never wanted to. In every successive film, even after *Baaz*, Guru Dutt would try to cast some other actor. We tried to persuade Shammi Kapoor to star in *Aar Paar*, and we took a camera test of Sunil Dutt for the role of

Preetam in *Mr & Mrs 55*. When all the arrangements were made, Guru Dutt couldn't sit idle and wait for the star to be available for shooting. He would feel restless, that's why he was forced to act in his own films. That's why he acted in *Baaz* .

We shot the film at Shrikant Studios near RK Studios in Chembur. We built a big boat in a *maidan* [open field] behind the studio, and we worked day and night. We took a lot of pains in *Baaz*, but the picture did not do well. Probably we hadn't paid enough attention to the special effects. For example, the ship in the scene on the high seas looked like a toy boat.

Baaz is set in the early 16th century. The Zamorin of Calicut refuses to allow the Portuguese to enter his state, and so the invaders settle along the Malabar coast. General Barbosa (played by K.N. Singh who had also acted in *Baazi* and *Jaal*) signs a treaty with the Queen (Sulochana Devi) of a small state. The treaty gives the Portuguese the right to trade, in exchange for providing military protection. With the help of the Queen's scheming nephew, Jaswant (actor Jaswant), General Barbosa soon begins to meddle in the affairs of the state. When he realizes that the local Muslim merchants control the state trade, he orders their persecution. Merchant Ramzan Ali and his friend Narayan Das are arrested. When Das's daughter Nisha (Geeta Bali) enters Barbosa's palace hoping to save her father, she is caught. Barbosa sells Nisha and her father to a cruel Portuguese pirate, Cabral (Ramsingh). While the pirate subjects Nisha to further humiliation on the high seas, Barbosa persuades Prince Ravi (Guru Dutt), the heir to the throne, to visit Portugal. Ravi's companion on the sea voyage is the scheming Rosita (Kuldeep Kaur), who tries desperately to seduce the young prince, but to no avail.

Nisha is witness to her father's murder and to the many atrocities committed by Cabral. She rouses her fellow slaves to mutiny. Cabral is killed, and Nisha becomes the new master of the 'Baaz', Cabral's vessel. Nisha's reputation as a much-feared pirate queen spreads as she pillages all Portuguese ships in sight, including the one bound for Portugal with Prince Ravi, Rosita and a court astrologer (Badruddin — credited as 'Johnny Walker' from this film onwards) on board. The royal party is taken prisoner, but Nisha spares their lives, remembering that Ravi had once rescued her from the Portuguese. Ravi joins the mutineers but does not reveal his true identity. Nisha and Ravi fall in love, and Ravi persuades her to return to land. Back on shore, Ravi hears that his cousin, the traitor Jaswant, is to be crowned king. When Ravi rushes to the palace, he is arrested. Nisha discovers Ravi's true identity and saves him from hanging. Nisha and Ravi join forces with other local chiefs and finally defeat Barbosa and his accomplices.

Guru Dutt's performance in *Baaz* is unremarkable. The moments when he seems most at ease are in dialogue with the frivolous Rosita, when we do see a glimpse of Guru Dutt's confident persona of *Aar Paar* and *Mr & Mrs 55*. Atmaram remembered that though Guru Dutt looked handsome in the film, the press was not favourable to him. Guru Dutt had originally wanted S.D. Burman to compose the film's music but when Burman refused the offer, Geeta Roy advised Guru Dutt to use O.P. Nayyar and Majrooh Sultanpuri instead. A striking example of O.P. Nayyar's contribution to the film is the song *Har zabaan ruki ruki, har nazar jhuki jhuki* (Silent tongues and lowered eyes) sung by Geeta Dutt. Through the song's stirring lyrics and dramatic music, Nisha encourages the pirate's slaves to mutiny. As the song builds to its climactic end, Ćabral is killed. Accompanied by the strains of a shrieking conch, Nisha stands proud and triumphant.

Interviews and articles featured over the years in *Filmfare* reveal that O.P. Nayyar was discovered by an HMV talent scout in 1945 when he was only seventeen and studying in Lahore. His composition for the song *Preetam aan milo* (Preetam/Beloved, come to me), originally sung by C.H. Atma on an HMV recording unconnected to any film and later used to wonderful effect in *Mr & Mrs 55*, was said to be written by Saroj Mohini whom Nayyar subsequently married. Though this first composition attracted immediate attention, Nayyar's name never made it to the record jacket.

In 1951, O.P. Nayyar moved from Amritsar to Bombay and began composing for films. Guru Dutt was unable to pay Nayyar his due for *Baaz* as the film had failed so dismally, but promised to offer him work on *Aar Paar*. *Baaz* was Nayyar's third film; his first contact with play-back singer Mohammed Rafi happened to be at the recording of a *Baaz* song, *Ghata men chupke bhi bijli jhalak dikhlaai jaati hai* (Though hidden in cloud, the lightning still shines through). Nayyar chose Talat Mahmood to sing the *Baaz* song *Mujhe dekho hasrat ki tasveer houn main* (Look at me, I am the very picture of desire), performed on screen by Guru Dutt. This is the only song that Talat Mahmood was to sing for Guru Dutt, who usually opted for play-back singers Mohammed Rafi and Hemant Kumar.

Besides the variety of music in *Baaz*, another point of interest in the film is the way Guru Dutt uses extended takes, particularly appropriate in the sequence in which Nisha reluctantly accepts that she is in love with Ravi. The scene has Nisha and Ravi in the lower deck of the ship as Ravi tries to convince her of his love. The camera is stationary as Nisha moves towards him and away from him as though she were trying to avoid the inevitability of falling in love. The entire sequence comprises only two shots, allowing the actors, and not the editing, to determine the pace of the scene. The intensity of their emotions reaches a dramatic peak in which nothing but their intimate world exists, and the sequence ends with a close-up of Nisha's eyes. The next time we see Nisha, the shot begins with a similar close-up of her eyes; this time when the camera pulls back, she is revealed looking through an old-fashioned telescope. These unusual moments are not, however, equalled by the overall impact of the film which suffers primarily from its dismal screenplay.

ATMARAM: *Baaz* was Guru Dutt's own idea. I worked a lot on the research for the film, but somehow it did not do well. The film's dialogues were written by Sarshar Sailani, who belonged to another era. Guru Dutt was a modern film-maker, but he was working at a time when there were still many old Urdu writers who had come from the stage. Naturally, Guru Dutt had to work with those writers in the beginning. There is a big.difference in writing for the stage and writing for films; so he had to struggle with them. They would bully him by refusing to write. Guru Dutt was young, he would just give up. I remember going to Sarshar Sailani's writing sessions. He had an assistant who would read out a single line of dialogue, sometimes thirty or forty times. He would repeat the same line until Sailani was inspired to add the second line. It was a play of words. *Baaz* was written like that. Those writers had no visual sense; they might have been strong on characterization and dialogues, but they certainly did not grasp the cinematic medium as Guru Dutt sensed it.

The frustrations that Guru Dutt had felt working with mediocre or inexperienced screenplay writers did not deter him from trying new genres. For a young director, who had made crime thrillers until that point in time, to take on a costume drama showed a curious spirit. Throughout his career, Guru Dutt never believed in depending on film formulae.

V.K. MURTHY: That was one of his greatest qualities: a thing which he liked today, he would not like tomorrow. So after *Jaal* came *Baaz*. The film was an utter flop. The producer Haridarshan Kaur got a bit upset — frightened rather — because they lost about a lakh and a half. I think Geeta Bali must have been earning around Rs 25,000

> per film. To lose a lakh and a half was a lot though it's nothing by today's standards. The story of *Baaz* was the story of a woman's rebellion against the Portuguese rulers. The emphasis should have been on action not romance. Guru Dutt made it into a love story. I told him that he was wrong to do that. I told him to make it an action film. But he was always firm about what he wanted to do, he was very determined. He wouldn't listen.

Following Guru Dutt's unsatisfactory experiences with a number of screen writers, he was fortunate to meet writer Abrar Alvi. Alvi, a young law graduate from Nagpur, had originally come to Bombay in the hope of becoming an actor. Alvi's cousin, whose screen name was Jaswant, was starring in *Baaz* and asked him to visit the sets. Jaswant (who also happened to be Geeta Bali's brother-in-law) introduced Alvi to Raj Khosla. When Raj Khosla discovered that Alvi was a writer, he asked him to re-write the dialogues of a scene in *Baaz*. Guru Dutt was very pleased with how Alvi improved on the original, and asked Alvi to work with him on his next film, *Aar Paar*. In a *Filmfare* interview (March, 1985), Abrar Alvi recalled that after seeing the rushes of *Baaz* and not liking it very much, he was asked by Guru Dutt what he thought of the film. Alvi replied by evading the issue: '*Aap bahut* photogenic *hain*' (You're very photogenic), to which Guru Dutt answered: '*Kuchh* actogenic *bhi hain ya nahin*' (Am I also a little actogenic or not?).

Abrar Alvi's contribution to Guru Dutt's work is immeasurable. Over the years, their friendship grew as they spent days and months together. Guru Dutt had at last found a writer who understood the cinema medium and who approached film writing with new energy and originality. Most Indian films, particularly the films of the forties, had all characters — whether prince or pauper — speaking in a uniform style of language. Alvi's particular talent was in scripting realistic and intelligent repartee and in giving each screen character his or her own individuality. All of Alvi's characters sound believable as they express themselves in a language reflecting their social and regional origins. Guru Dutt's naturalism derives in part from this realistic use of colloquial speech.

Abrar Alvi has a deep and sonorous speaking voice. His stressed intonation creating a dramatic mood that brings back the actor in him, he becomes Rustom of *Aar Paar* or Preetam of *Mr & Mrs 55* as he remembers his closest and dearest friend:

Guru Dutt was always lost in his work. I remember the Maharajah of Baroda coming to visit the sets of *Baaz*. He was accompanied by some British ladies. I could tell that Guru Dutt felt that he had to be courteous, but he never liked being distracted from his work. In his situation, anyone else would have bent over backwards for the Maharajah, but Guru Dutt spoke to him for a few minutes and then said: 'Excuse me', and went back to filming.

Guru Dutt was impatient to marry Geeta Roy and is said to have taken her to the Haji Malang Baba shrine in Kalyan to ask whether she intended to marry him or the Bengali boy whom her family favoured. Finally Guru Dutt and Geeta married on May 26, 1953 — nearly three years after becoming engaged.

LALITHA LAJMI: Guru Dutt and Geeta got married in the traditional Bengali style at Geeta's mother's home in Santa Cruz [a Bombay suburb]. On the morning of the 26th, some of Geeta's Bengali friends came to Guru Dutt's flat at 12th Road in Khar with a plate full of flowers, *diyas* [lamps], and *chandan* paste [sandalwood paste] to give the bridegroom the ceremonial bath. They applied *chandan* paste on Guru Dutt's forehead — it's supposed to be auspicious — while one of the ladies blew a conch shell and garlanded him. The wedding is usually performed in the evening for Bengalis, so the actual *Saptapadi* ceremony [in which the bride and groom circle the fire seven times] took place late at night. Among Saraswats, the ceremony is called *Godhuli Lagna* which means wedding at sunset.

Geeta was dressed in a red brocade Benares sari; she looked stunningly beautiful. She had *chandan* paste dots on her forehead and *sindoor* [vermilion] and all the jewellery. Guru Dutt was dressed in a white silk kurta and a dhoti worn in the Bengali-style. They looked a lovely pair, and they looked very happy. The bridal bed was decorated with flowers, and all the gifts of saris and jewellery that Geeta's mother gave her were on display. For me it was the first time that I saw such glitter and pomp; I still remember the shehnai playing and the sound of conch shells blowing that night.

Three days later, Atma and I went to their house to bring Geeta home with us. Amma placed all the traditional *diyas* and rice in a plate with *kumkum* [red powder] and flowers at the door step. When Geeta arrived, Amma performed *aarti* and applied *kumkum* to her forehead and sprinkled rice three times on her forehead. Geeta then stepped into our home and family.

The wedding was a grand affair attended by many leading personalities of the film world including Dev Anand, Vyjayantimala,

Nutan and Motilal. But differences in Guru Dutt and Geeta's backgrounds and social standing appeared to cause difficulties. Geeta Dutt was a leading play-back singer at the time while Guru Dutt had yet to establish himself as director. The situation was further aggravated by rumours in the press suggesting that Guru Dutt had only married Geeta for her money. Vasanthi Padukone remembers feeling apprehensive about the marriage almost immediately after the wedding; but her memoirs (*Imprint*, 1979) show that she dismissed the press rumours about Guru Dutt's motivations:

> The wedding took place with great pomp! It was a sensation in the film industry at the time. But people, as well as relatives, said that Guru Dutt married Geeta because of her money and because of the big name she had in the industry... Guru Dutt never yearned for wealth. I think he never even glanced at Geeta's jewellery. In spite of his earlier hardships, he never hoarded money. He had already bought a two-seater sports car himself. He did not take what Geeta earned, nor did he ask her how she spent her money...
>
> On July 9, 1954, on Guru Dutt's birthday, a son (Tarun) was born to them... After Tarun was born, everything went smoothly. There were tussles between them, but Guru Dutt loved his son. He and Geeta were happy at times. Among his three children, Tarun was his favourite.

H.G. Films announced two others productions to be directed by Guru Dutt and starring Geeta Bali: one a film called 'BMT 112' which — by the look of its publicity material showing a taxi-driver at his wheel — became *Aar Paar*, and the other entitled 'Geetanjali' which never materialized in any form. The financial loss incurred in *Baaz* meant that Guru Dutt and Haridarshan Kaur went their separate ways. Guru Dutt was at last independent, free to make the kind of films that most interested him, starting with *Aar Paar*.

CHAPTER SIX

Aar Paar

In 1953, Guru Dutt created his own company, Guru Dutt Productions (later renamed Guru Dutt Films Private Ltd), through which he produced all his subsequent films. The company originally had three shareholders: Atmaram, Guruswamy and Guru Dutt himself. Guru Dutt Productions' first film *Aar Paar* was released at Novelty Cinema, Bombay on May 7, 1954.

Aar Paar is the story of a Bombay taxi-driver, Kalu Birju (Guru Dutt), who is sentenced to prison for speeding. Kalu is released two months before his term is completed for good behaviour. As Kalu is about to leave the prison, a cell-mate asks him to deliver a message to Captain, the owner of a hotel. On the day of his release, Kalu visits his old employer (Rashid Khan) who refuses to let Kalu drive his taxi again. Kalu wanders on the streets when he accidentally meets Nikki (Shyama), the daughter of a garage-owner, and helps to fix her car. For Kalu, it is love at first sight. A street urchin, Elaichi (Jagdeep), is witness to Kalu's courting and is highly amused. Kalu returns home to find that his brother-in-law does not want an ex-convict in his house, and Kalu finds himself out on the streets. He finds a friend in young Elaichi who teaches him how to live rough on the streets. Kalu visits the hotel to deliver the message to Captain, and meets a cabaret dancer, (Shakila), and Rustom, a Parsee barman (Johnny Walker). Kalu finds his way to Nikki's garage, and meets her father (Jagdish Sethi), the stern but kind-hearted Punjabi garage-owner. The garage-owner takes pity on the unemployed Kalu, gives him a job as mechanic and allows him to sleep in the garage. Nikki and Kalu's love flourishes among broken car engines and old worn-out tires. When Nikki's father discovers their romancing, he promptly throws Kalu out. Homeless and jobless, Kalu turns to Captain and his band of crooks for a job. Captain is busy planning a bank robbery and thinks that Kalu might be useful in driving the getaway car (a taxi). The cabaret dancer takes a fancy to Kalu who seems content to be distracted by her, as Nikki — too scared to oppose her father's wishes — refuses to elope with him. The dancer soon realizes that Kalu loves only Nikki, and seeks her revenge. She persuades Captain to have Nikki kidnapped. With Rustom's help, Kalu manages to rescue Nikki and prove himself a true hero. Nikki's father is now happy to give his daughter's hand in marriage.

Aar Paar's success was immediate, though the film is said to have irritated some of the more conservative who, like Nikki's father, disapproved of Kalu's low social status and his blatant disdain for bourgeois values. Kalu declares that his position in the world is a matter of circumstance rather than class. He has ambitions to equal the middle-class Nikki. In a delightfully comic scene, we see Kalu one evening after work in the garage, trying to learn English (perhaps as a means to better his situation). Nikki corrects his pronunciation of the word 'girl' and he answers: 'Thank you very much kindly.' Lalitha Lajmi once recalled that Nikki's character is likely to have been based on Amarjeet, a Punjabi girl whom Guru Dutt knew during the years the Padukones lived in Calcutta. The young Sikh girl's father happened to own a garage, and disapproved of his daughter's friendship with Guru Dutt. Guru Dutt's youngest brother Vijay Padukone, who now produces and directs television serializations, also believes that things that happened in Guru Dutt's life have been re-worked in all his films:

> I always noticed that the family matters that disgusted Guru Dutt were usually brought up during meal-times when he was eating his food. Sometimes it was my parents arguing: Guru Dutt would leave his plate, wash his hands, take his packet of Gold Flake cigarettes and go out for a walk. There is a scene like that in *Pyaasa*, and even in *Aar Paar*. When Kalu returns home to his sister and she feeds him, his brother-in-law comes in and complains about his presence. Kalu walks out.

The plot of the film may now seem formulaic ('poor boy overcomes social barriers to win his beloved'), and the film's ending involving a long car chase and shoot-out accompanied to the music of Sheherezade is comical and hackneyed. Yet Guru Dutt brings to *Aar Paar* a freshness and a light-heartedness which lend distinction to the film. The film's great strength lies in the way Guru Dutt develops personalities out of minor characters. These ordinary people who carry the interest of the film — a taxi driver, a barman, a newspaper vendor — all shine with their individual wit and integrity. The world inhabited by Kalu and his friends reflects the mores of city living where personal adaptability and capacity to balance the traditional with the modern are essential traits. The screenplay of the film was written by Nabendu Ghosh and the dialogues by Abrar Alvi. Abrar Alvi also suggested the title of the film to Guru Dutt and because the title *Aar Paar* (literally, 'This side or that') had no meaningful connection to the narrative of the film, Alvi wrote a special scene to provide such a contextual link. When Nikki cannot decide whether to elope with Kalu or stay with her father, Kalu says, 'Let's toss a coin — *aar ya paar* (heads or tails).' The words of the title are also integrated into the song, *Kabhi aar kabhi paar laaga teer-e-nazar* (Your arrow-like glances strike all over, sometimes this side, sometimes that).

ABRAR ALVI: As a college student, I used to get very irritated by the way film dialogues were written in those days. The writer's own personal language was imposed on all the screen characters. There was no real sense of characterization, and dialogues were theatrical and chaste. It was book language, not everyday spoken language. I used to think to myself that if I ever had the chance to write for films, I would use the kind of language that is appropriate to each character. Is the character a villager, is he educated, is he sophisticated, what kind of person is he? Where does he come from — Punjab, Gujarat, or U.P.? I wanted language to reflect his reality, to give an illusion of reality. Complete realism is not possible in films.

I believe that we started a trend of modern writing with *Aar Paar*, and Guru Dutt backed me all the way. We gave each character individuality. For example, the hero, Kalu, is from Madhya Pradesh, so he speaks in a particular style. When referring to himself, Kalu does not say '*my* state' he says, 'your friend's state' (*yaaron ka haal*). Kalu isn't educated or highly cultured, so his language reflects his social status. The garage-owner in the film is from Punjab, so he speaks in Punjabi slang. I added some colour to the style in which each character speaks.

All the characters in *Aar Paar* have real presence. One never forgets the smiling Elaichi, or Rustom, the fast-talking Parsee barman, or Rustom's future mother-in-law, played by one of the rare comediennes of Hindi cinema, Uma Devi or 'Tun Tun', who became another regular in the Guru Dutt team. Uma Devi had begun her career as a play-back singer; her most famous song *Afsaana likh rahi houn* (I write this story), in the 1947 film *Dard* led to further recording opportunities.

When Uma Devi decided to abandon her singing career, music director Naushad suggested that she work as a comedienne and exploit her natural flair for comedy. Her screen name derives from her first screen role as the comic character Tun Tun in the film *Babul*. In an interview in *The Illustrated Weekly of India* in April 1987, Tun Tun commented that it was only Guru Dutt who insisted on crediting her in his films under her real name. She added that her favourite role was as a Christian landlady in *Mr & Mrs 55* — a role that she found particularly easy to portray because she lived in Mahim, an area of Bombay where many of her neighbours and friends were Christian.

When Guru Dutt completed the first two reels of *Aar Paar*, he showed them to some film distributors who expressed reservations about Dutt's own performance as Kalu. Guru Dutt immediately asked Shammi Kapoor (Geeta Bali's husband and a rising star of the time) to replace him. Shammi Kapoor insisted on seeing the edited reels of the film, and pretended not to have the time to work in *Aar Paar*, believing that Guru Dutt was perfectly adequate in the role. Guru Dutt's confidence in the film is remarkably different from his hesitant performance in *Baaz*. Guru Dutt brings a hint of the Chaplinesque to the role of Kalu. In addition to the typical Chaplin-style short, upturned trousers that Kalu wears on his release from prison, the similarities in his marginal life-style, sleeping at nights in the doorways of closed shops, are clearly reminiscent of Chaplin's tramp persona.

Geeta Bali was first considered for the role of Nikki, but when she pulled out of the film, Geeta Dutt suggested that Shyama take the part. Shyama started her career in her own name (Khurshid Akhtar) as 'Baby Khurshid' when she was only nine years old, appearing in the famous *qawali* scene in the 1944 film *Zeenat*. Director Vijay Bhatt gave her the screen name of Shyama as he felt there were already too many actresses named Khurshid working in films.

SHYAMA: In 1953, I had twenty movies in hand. I was very busy and didn't have time to work in *Aar Paar*. But Geeta Dutt came personally to see me and said that Guru Dutt had me in mind for the role of Nikki. I went to his office and he told me the outline of the story. I liked the role and thought to myself this would be a good opportunity to work with this fine actor and director. We shot the film in Shrikant Studios in Chembur. Guru Dutt was a romantic really, and Geeta was very possessive. She would come to the sets and used to keep an eye on him. That made me laugh.

Guru Dutt was an all-rounder. He used to tell us how to act, how to laugh, how to dance, how to pull faces. As an actor, he was confident but unless he was satisfied, he would shoot take after take. He was a very helpful person. He would tell us what he wanted shot by shot. In those days there weren't any dance directors, and he would show us the movement. Basically, he was a good dancer. I remember in the song, *Sun sun sun sun zaalima* (Listen, you cruel one), he got the camera whirling around us. There was nothing on that set, just a car in a garage.

As in many of Guru Dutt's films, the hero in *Aar Paar* is loved by two women. The woman that Kalu loves is respectable in the eyes of the world, but unable to overcome social barriers. The other woman in Kalu's life, the cabaret dancer, is disdained by society and is a more complex and embittered person. When Kalu rejects her, she turns vengeful in the manner of vamp stereotypes. Guru Dutt chose the young actress Shakila for the role of the cabaret dancer. Shakila did not go on to a long career in films, deciding to retire in 1961 when she married and travelled abroad. Shakila's sister, Noor, who had also worked with Guru Dutt, married Johnny Walker.

SHAKILA: Guru Dutt used to explain things well to us artistes. He was very mild, and patient. But he'd get angry when he didn't get what he wanted. Then he would be very picky. There was a scene in which I had to look down and then fling my head back. We had five or six retakes. He wanted me to look exactly the way he had imagined. He was particular about the way my hair fell. I didn't have the chance to work with him again, but I did act in Raj Khosla's *C.I.D.* which was produced by Guru Dutt.

The first day I worked with Guru Dutt for *Aar Paar* involved a song sequence. I went to the sets, a room with cardboard boxes lying everywhere. It looked like nothing. Everyone asked Guru Dutt how he could possibly film there. But he did. The song was, *Houn abhi main jawan* (I am still young) and how fantastically he picturized it.

Guru Dutt's talent in picturizing songs had always impressed his colleagues with its originality. Breaking away from the usual patterns, Guru Dutt allowed a wider range of screen characters, other than the hero and heroine, to express themselves in song. The fact that almost anyone could sing in his films introduces an element of surprise, a moment of unpredictability such as when a female construction worker (Kum Kum, who from *Aar Paar* onwards often featured in minor roles in Guru Dutt's films), never to be seen again in the film, sings *Kabhi aar kabhi paar laaga teer-e-nazar*. In this instance, the lively song acts as a commentary describing Kalu's feelings as he falls in love with Nikki.

In all his films, Guru Dutt attempts to make the song work as an extension of dialogue. In many cases, the song has as much dramatic weight as expression through dialogue. Guru Dutt's son, Tarun, would always smilingly say, 'To miss a song in my father's films is missing a transition in the narrative.'

In an interview in *Filmfare* (January 1987), O.P. Nayyar commented that it was Guru Dutt who had insisted that Nayyar base some of his *Aar Paar* compositions on western melodies. *Sun sun sun sun zaalima* was allegedly inspired by Bing Crosby's 'Sing sing sing a song with me'. Guru Dutt's choices of western tunes were not only American but also included a popular Spanish song of the fifties, *Quizas quizas quizas* (Perhaps) which found its Indianized version in *Babuji dheere chalna* (Mister, tread softly). Whether the music was borrowed or not, the success of *Aar Paar*'s songs helped establish O.P. Nayyar as one of the leading music directors of the time. The Urdu poet and lyricist, Majrooh Sultanpuri, who has often worked with Nayyar, wrote the lyrics for the film. Sultanpuri has worked with the best and the worst directors of Indian film. Unsure of his date of birth in Azamgarh, Uttar Pradesh, Majrooh guesses it to be either 1919 or 1920. In January 1946, he came to Bombay with his mentor, the poet Jigar Muradabadi, to participate in a *mushaira* (poetry symposium). His poetry was so well appreciated by all those present (including the celebrated director/producer A.R. Kardar, who subsequently offered Majrooh a contract to join Kardar Films on a monthly salary of Rs 500), that Majrooh decided to join films and stay on in Bombay abandoning his life as a *hakim*. The first film Sultanpuri wrote for was *Shahjehan* with Naushad's music. The film included the famous songs *Gham diye mustaqil* and *Jab dil hi toot gaya* sung by singing star K.L. Saigal, performing in what was to be Saigal's penultimate film.

Majrooh's songs in Mehboob Khan's *Andaaz* in 1949 earned him a place among the leading lyricists of the time such as Shailendra, Sahir Ludhianvi, Rajinder Krishan, and Shakeel Badayuni. For his rebellious writing and his involvement with the Communist cause, Majrooh was jailed for two years (1950-1952) in a cramped cell at the Arthur Road prison in Bombay, along with IPTA member Balraj Sahni. When Majrooh was released, after completing the full jail term, he went back to song-writing and poetry.

Majrooh Sultanpuri's stern manner is more telling of his reluctance to suffer fools than of his true nature. He may appear severe, but his laughter reveals a generosity of spirit. His house is full of daughters,

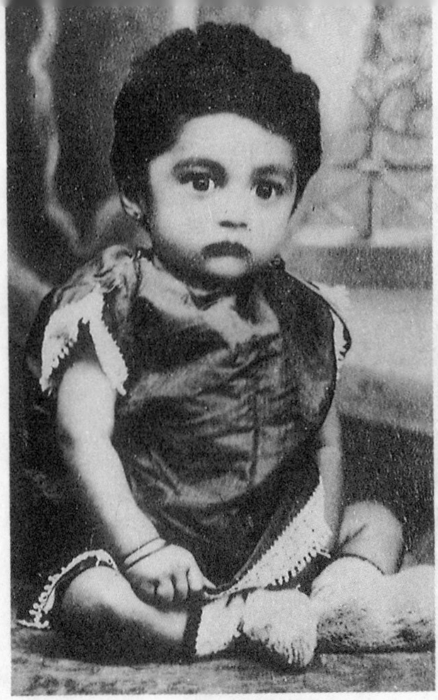

Guru Dutt Padukone at 14 months,
Bangalore 1926

(L to R) Shivshankar Padukone, Guru Dutt, Lalitha, Vasanthi Padukone
and Atmaram in B.B.Benegal's garden, Calcutta 1937

Guru Dutt, a cousin, Lalitha and Atmaram in B.B.Benegal's garden, Calcutta 1937

Sudarshan Benegal, B.B.Benegal, Guru Dutt and another member of the Benegal family, Calcutta late 1930s

Guru Dutt learns dance at Uday Shankar's India Cultural Centre in Almora from 1942 to 1944

The painting by B.B.Benegal that inspired the young Guru Dutt's 'snake dance'

Guru Dutt performing his 'snake dance' in Eden Gardens, Calcutta 1940

Dev Anand and Geeta Bali in Guru Dutt's first film (*Baazi*)

Geeta Bali in *Baazi*: the dances were choreographed by Zohra Sehgal whom Guru Dutt met in his Almora days

Geeta Roy, playback singer,
surrounded by fans

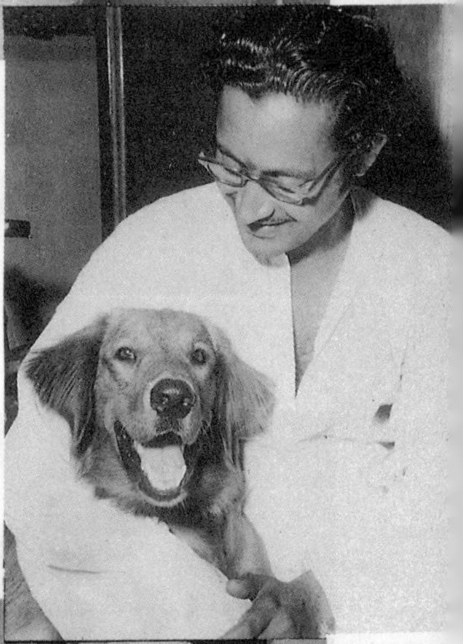

Guru Dutt with his golden retriever,
Tony, named after *Jaal*'s hero. 1952

Nagam, Geeta, Vijay, Shivshankar and Vasanthi Padukone, Guru Dutt,
Devi, and Atmaram at Lalitha's wedding, Bombay, December 1952

Geeta Bali and Dev Anand in Guru Dutt's second film, *Jaal*

Guru Dutt and Geeta Bali on location for *Baaz* (released in April 1953)

Guru Dutt in his first lead role, as Prince Ravi in *Baaz*

Geeta Bali and Geeta Roy on the sets of *Baaz*

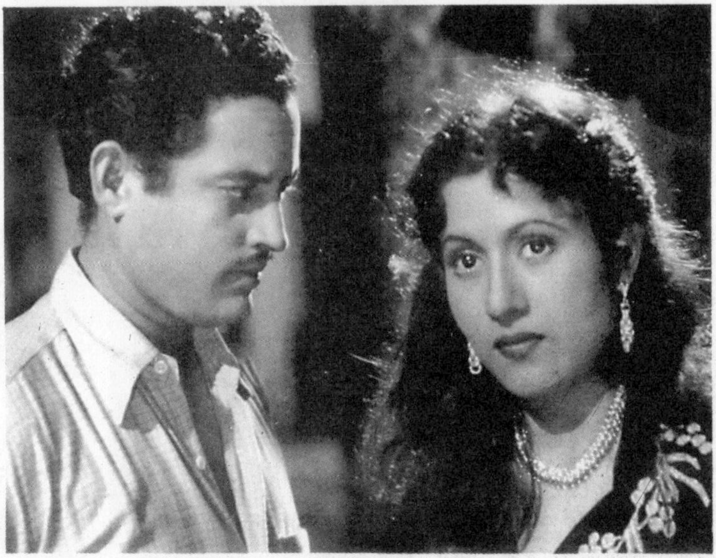

Guru Dutt and Madhubala in *Mr & Mrs 55* written by Abrar Alvi

Guru Dutt and Madhubala (*Mr & Mrs 55*)

Abrar Alvi in his Juhu home, Bombay 1989
(Photograph: Peter Chappell)

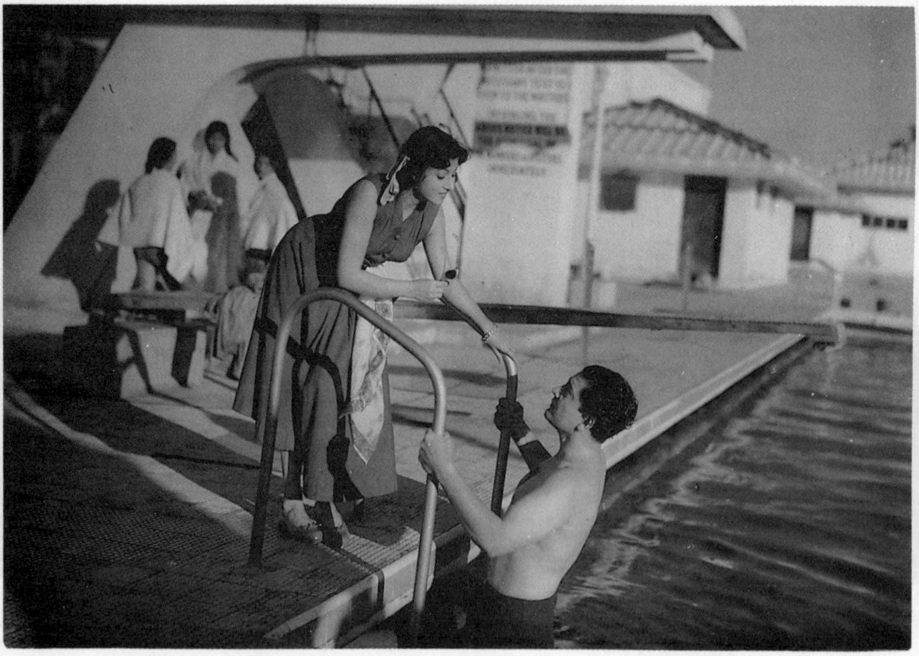

Mahatma Gandhi Swimming Pool in Shivaji Park, Bombay location for *Mr & Mrs 55*

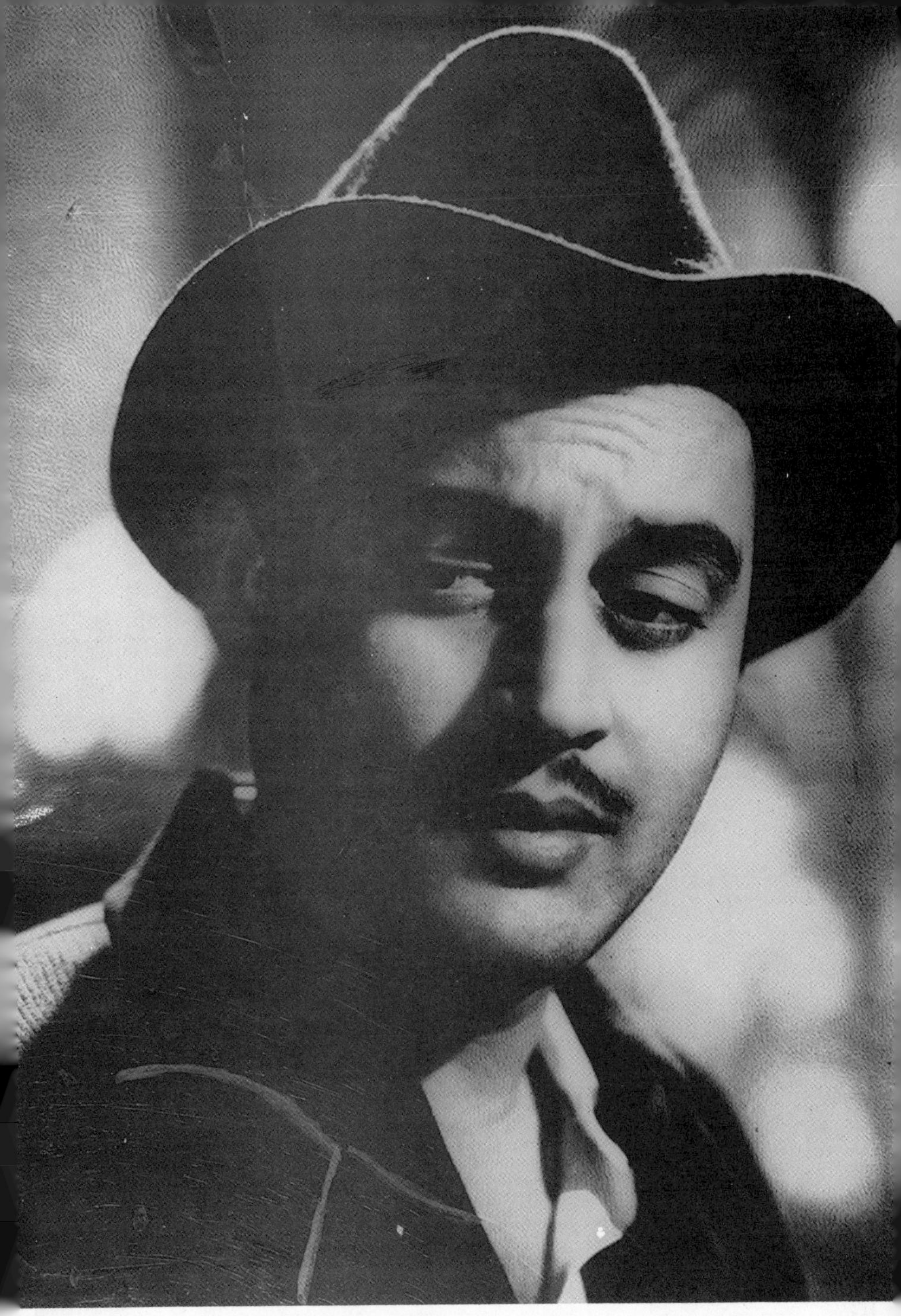

Guru Dutt as the unemployed cartoonist Preetam (*Mr & Mrs 55*)

Dev Anand and Waheeda Rehman in her first Hindi film role (*C.I.D.*)

Publicity still from the rarely seen *Sailaab* directed by Guru Dutt

Raj Khosla in his Bombay office, 1989 (Photograph: Peter Chappell)

Guru Dutt as Vijay (*Pyaasa*)

Johnny Walker originally cast as the treacherous Shyam (*Pyaasa*)

Waheeda Rehman and Mala Sinha as Gulab and Meena haggle over the price of integrity (*Pyaasa*)

Guru Dutt as the poet Vijay (*Pyaasa*)

Waheeda Rehman and Guru Dutt in a publicity still for *Pyaasa*

sons, daughters-in-law, and grandchildren. He wears impeccable white *kurtas* and is addicted to *paan*. Majrooh remembers the long hours that Guru Dutt and he spent working together. He remembers the young director as a decent, cultured and creative man who always treated all his colleagues, whether music director or light-boy, as equals. His intelligence, compassion and wit become apparent as he speaks gladly of Guru Dutt:

> When we worked together, Guru Dutt would sit with me and the music director. He would start by explaining the story to us. Then he'd describe the situation in which the song would appear. The music director would give me the tune. Guru Dutt also had a great sense for music. He would describe the vocabulary used in dialogues by his screen characters. He would always make sure that the songs that I wrote would correspond to the vocabulary his characters used. I would ask him, 'What time of day does the song take place? Where is the hero sitting? Is it in a village, a city or in a town? What is the hero's social standing? What sort of people does he mix with?' Songwriters ask these questions — at least they should! Guru Dutt would answer very patiently. If there was a difference of opinion, I would argue stubbornly and if he wanted to win me over, he would laugh and say, 'Come on, stop arguing.'
>
> In those days, most scripts would be written and divided into scenes — perhaps there would be 112 or 120 scenes in a given film. Then we would decide where the songs would feature. Various things had to be taken into consideration. For example, one had to allow a certain time gap between one song and another. When a song is properly used it is like a scene in itself. Many romantic feelings do not sound as effective in prose as they do in song. Romantic feelings are more effective if you express them musically and poetically. That is the role of the song. It should not repeat what the dialogue has already stated. Guru Dutt always wanted the song to carry the narrative forward, and that his songs be an integral part of the screenplay.
>
> I remember for *Aar Paar*, I wrote the song *Sun sun sun sun zaalima, pyaar mujhko tujhse ho gaya*. Guru Dutt said, 'I don't like it, the words should be lighter — use *humko tumse pyaar ho gaya* — the notes will be more easy-going.' But I said, 'That's grammatically wrong. You can only say *"tumse"* if you use the plural *suno suno*. I still remember the way Guru Dutt said, *'Are yaar, Majrooh, chhodo na, gaana sunne ki cheez hoti hai, itna kaun wahaan tumhaara grammar leke baithega* (Oh come on Majrooh, forget it — a song is a thing to be listened to, who is going to

bother about your grammar?)' The song was a big hit, even though there is a grammatical fault in it.

The popularity and appeal of many Indian film songs often have nothing to do with the film in which they feature. In the minds of the audiences songs become disassociated from the characters who perform them on screen. Yet it is true to say that the songs in Guru Dutt's films are rarely separate from the personalities who enact them on screen. Audiences will always associate *Mohabbat kar lo, ji bhar lo, aji kisne roka hai* (Fall in love if you must, who's stopping you?) with the mildly cynical Kalu, or *Sar jo tera chakaraaye* (If your head reels with pain) with Abdul Sattar, the head masseur of *Pyaasa.*

The use of a song within the narrative is considered to break the illusion of realism in cinema. Guru Dutt was well aware of this and, despite his great talent for song picturization, often wrote of feeling constrained in having to include songs in his films. Because popular Hindi cinema does not see music and dance as separate from storytelling and is entirely dependent on songs as essential ingredients, individual directors have needed to develop their skills in this specialized area of Indian film making. By insisting that Majrooh Sultanpuri use a vocabulary appropriate to his characters in *Aar Paar*, Kalu and Rustom became more believable. Guru Dutt seemed particularly interested in creating a realistic mood for a song, not only through language, but also in his choice of locations. Many directors choose to enhance the fantasy elements of a song by situating it in an unreal setting. Songs often take place in locations that are unconnected to the space in which the characters of a film are seen to otherwise exist. Guru Dutt, however, nearly always chose to situate his songs within the space inhabited by his characters. A fine example is the love-duet, *Sun sun sun sun zaalima,* set in the stark and unromantic garage with a car providing the centre-piece as the two lovers circle around each other within this restricted space in a brilliantly simple piece of balletic movement. Beyond considerations of language and space, the songs in Guru Dutt's work appear better integrated than in most Indian films. Though many critics and admirers have observed Guru Dutt's skill in this area, Majrooh Sultanpuri's analysis has particular insight:

> Guru Dutt looked out for two things in a song: the lyrics of a song should not have any opening music, and secondly, the song must not be dull. If a song has a long introductory tune that leads to the first line of the song, the audiences think to themselves, 'Let's sit back, here comes a song.' Audiences know that once the

> music has started, a song is bound to take over. But Guru Dutt would cut straight from dialogue to the first line of the song. In this way, he made the song work as a direct extension of dialogue.
>
> On the second point, I think he was the only director in those days who made sure that the song had pace. He gave that great importance. The words of the song might be of interest, the musical interlude as well, but he made sure that a song had feeling and visual appeal. Take the song I wrote for *Mr & Mrs 55*, *Chal diye banda nawaaz chhedkar mere dil ka saaz* (The master leaves, touching the strings of my heart). He filmed it by a village river bank where young washer-women are drying saris. The saris are blowing in the wind. The song is so visual and so pleasing to the eye. Many people copy him but he was the first to make the song visually interesting. His greatest talent was his consistency. His songs were always on a higher level, they had impact. He gave them much thought, he'd spend nights thinking of song situations.

Many of the songs featuring in Guru Dutt's work are integrated into the narrative in the way described by Majrooh Sultanpuri. In *Aar Paar*, Kalu overhears a sugary dialogue between two lovers as they ride in his taxi. Kalu himself is disillusioned with love. Following their spoken declarations of undying affection, he reacts in song, *Mohabbat kar lo, ji bhar lo, aji kis ne roka hai, par bare ghazab ki baat hai is main bhi dhoka hai* (Fall in love if you must, who's stopping you? But strange as it may seem, love is full of treachery). When Guru Dutt does choose a long passage of opening music, the role of that particular song seems precisely to highlight fantasy as separate from reality. Vijay of *Pyaasa* has a day-dream of idyllic love, so the duet, *Hum aap ki ankhon main* (If I were to make my heart dwell in your eyes) has a long opening musical phrase, quite uncharacteristic of the other songs in the film. This love-duet is distinctly different, not only in the musical structure of the song, but also in Guru Dutt's choice of setting. Unlike the many scenes and songs of *Pyaasa* shot on the streets of Calcutta, in this duet, the heroine Meena descends a staircase that seems to come straight from the heavens, while the hero Vijay dressed in fine attire is enveloped by a rising mist as he awaits his beloved.

Aar Paar was released at the Novelty Cinema in Bombay on May 7, 1954. *Filmindia*'s review of the film (July 1954) calls it, 'a fast and furious entertainer' and adds:

> The picture has a remarkable resemblance — call it accidental or incidental — to the Hollywood picture *Drive A Crooked Road*. Achieving this resemblance must be considered the work of a

> genius seeing that Hollywood is thousands of miles away and Guru Dutt is too busy to see foreign pictures when they are released in Bombay. That is one good thing about crime. Its conception is common to all humanity. All one needs is a natural genius for it. Guru Dutt however has produced *Aar Paar* with such an accent on entertainment, making the crime content incidental, that the picture does become quite enjoyable with its fast and furious action. Production values are quite good. Sets range from effective to ridiculous. Photography is quite pleasing and there is a rare sense of harmony in cameraman Murthy's work... Guru Dutt's direction is quite smooth for his limited purpose of entertaining without straining the mind.

Raj Khosla remembers that reviews and criticisms did not affect Guru Dutt very much:

> Guru Dutt never bothered about critics. He was his own critic. He knew where he was going wrong and he would say, 'Raj, this film is going wrong, this film will not go over right — *yeh gadbad ho gayi hai* (this has gone wrong)'. He could feel it.

CHAPTER SEVEN

Mr & Mrs 55

In 1954, Guru Dutt and his young family moved to a five-room flat in an apartment block called Seth Nivas on 16th Road in the same Bombay suburban area of Khar. He bought a small farm and some land in Lonavla (near Poona) where he did some farming. He would often leave Bombay when his work schedule allowed it, preferring the solitude of the farm to the glamorous film world. Guru Dutt's personality seems to have undergone a change at this time. From the outgoing man who enjoyed family picnics and social gatherings, he became more solitary, enjoying only his work and the company of those who worked with him.

ATMARAM: The way Guru Dutt lived! I don't think that he was meant for a normal married life. He should have lived like someone in France, where you live with someone and are not necessarily married to them. But Guru Dutt was also tied to tradition. It wasn't a question of unfaithfulness, it was more than that. He felt no responsibility towards his family, or towards society in any manner. He would not attend any parties or family functions. Geeta was a sociable sort, it was very difficult for her. When he was in his twenties and thirties, he worked round the clock. If he'd feel like going away, he would take his car and go straight from the studio to Lonavla without informing anyone. So there were a lot of misunderstandings. Geeta was a very good person, very talented; but intellectually they were not matched.

He was quite social in his early days. In fact, he was such a good assistant that everybody wanted him. Director Banerji wanted him, Gyan Mukherjee wanted him. Guru Dutt had a very pleasant nature. People were friendly with him. Whether it was the success or his filmmaking, he became increasingly enclosed, more and more cut off.

Vasanthi Padukone writes in her memoirs of the events following the success of *Aar Paar* (*Imprint*, 1979):

> Guru Dutt bought some land at Lonavla to do some farming. There he built a cosy two-room flat with all facilities. He loved a quiet life. Whenever he felt depressed or had time on his hands, he used to go and spend a few days there. Sometimes he took his script-writer [Abrar Alvi] with him. A couple was engaged to look after the farm. He would ask them to prepare *bajra roti* and hot chutney which he loved. Sometimes he would cook *khichdi*, serve the workers and himself... In 1955, Guru Dutt started his next film, *Mr & Mrs 55*. The heroine was Madhubala, and Guru Dutt played the hero. It was a semi-comedy and became a hit.

Mr & Mrs 55 is the story of an impoverished cartoonist, Preetam (Guru Dutt), who relies on his photographer friend, Johnny (Johnny Walker), to save him from creditors and impending starvation. Preetam, who is desperately looking for work as a cartoonist, encounters the beautiful Anita (Madhubala) at a tennis match. Anita is virtually controlled by her aunt Sita Devi (Lalitha Pawar), a crusader for women's rights who means to protect Anita from men. Anita's father, however, wishes to see her married and stipulates in his will that she will only inherit his fortune if she is married within a month of her twenty-first birthday. Sita Devi plans to contrive a marriage which will be immediately followed by divorce, thereby fulfilling the terms of the will while also preserving Anita's independence. Unaware that Preetam is already in love with her niece Anita, Sita Devi arranges for him to marry her, making it clear that once married Preetam must not see Anita and must divorce her when instructed.

When Anita discovers that Preetam has agreed to be the hired husband, he falls in her esteem. Preetam and Anita marry, 1955-style: far from the traditional ritual held in a *mandap*, their marriage takes place at breakneck speed in a Bombay registry office to the accompaniment of a racy jazz sound-track. Preetam, frustrated at not being allowed to meet Anita, decides to carry her off to his brother's home in a nearby village. Anita is deeply moved by Preetam's traditional sister-in-law (Kum Kum) and the simplicity with which she lives and loves. However, Anita has already sent for Sita Devi to rescue her. Preetam believes that Anita does not love him and provides Sita Devi with evidence that will help to bring about the divorce. A trial follows in which Preetam's character is maligned. Before the court arrives at its decision, Anita realizes that she loves Preetam and wants to stay married to him. When Anita declares to her aunt that a woman's happiness is not found in the freedom advocated by westernized women but lies in traditional marriage, the furious Sita Devi locks her up in her room. In the meantime, Preetam prepares to leave Bombay to live in Delhi. Anita escapes from her aunt's home with the help of Johnny and his girl-friend, and rushes to the airport to stop Preetam from leaving. *Mr & Mrs 55* ends in fairy-tale style with Preetam and Anita united at last.

Though the film is essentially a satirical comedy, it is Guru Dutt's first film to introduce — in a more definitive way than in his previous work — a concern for social realities. *Mr & Mrs 55* opposes the corrupt influence of westernization on India's urban rich by reaffirming traditional Indian values. The film's greatest weakness — which also dates it — is its highly reactionary and simplistic view of women struggling for independence. Sita Devi is a caricature, portrayed as a villain rather than as a serious crusader for womens' rights. The film's greatest strength is its use of intelligent repartee rather than the usual buffoonery and slapstick prevalent in many Hindi comedies. *Mr & Mrs 55* has much of the pace, mood and feel of the American comedy, and is probably the most Hollywood-influenced of all Guru Dutt's work.

ABRAR ALVI: When I was a student at Nagpur university, I wrote a play called *Modern Marriage*. I narrated the play to Guru Dutt. He liked it a lot and said, 'Abrar, let's make a film with this.' He asked me to add a twist to the plot which wasn't in the original play — he talked about some American film starring Cary Grant and Bette Davis, in which she is a European who must marry an American citizen so that she can stay in America. She decides to marry Cary Grant, an unemployed actor, on the condition that they will divorce as soon as her right of domicile is established. We took this twist from the Bette Davis film, and we added the women's liberation angle ourselves.

In *Mr & Mrs 55*, there is a scene in which Sita Devi confronts Preetam on his views. She says, '*Tum communist ho*?' (Are you a communist?). He replies, '*Ji nahin, cartoonist*' (No, a cartoonist). The repartee is fired back at great speed, it's a phonetic punning on the words. But there is some thought behind it too. That style of repartee was my forte. Humour has become very loud in Indian films. In those days, subtle humour was appreciated.

In one another scene, I had decided that the hero, Preetam, would only say the word 'Yes' throughout the exchange of dialogue with Sita Devi. But each time he would say '*ji haan*' [yes] it would take on another meaning. The situation is that Preetam is upset because he isn't allowed to see Anita, the woman he has married and loves. The villain of the piece is her aunt, Sita Devi. So Preetam draws a cartoon. That cartoon was actually drawn by India's top cartoonist, R.K. Laxman; it is his hand that you see in the frame, and the drawing was his idea too. Sita Devi appears in the cartoon wearing a Roman toga and stands in a Roman chariot with a whip in one hand. She holds the whip like a torch of liberty. Anita and Preetam, who are on all fours, are the horses that pull the chariot. Once we had that drawing, we conceived the next scene.

Sita Devi sees the cartoon printed in the newspaper. She enters Preetam's room with the newspaper in her hand. She is absolutely furious.

Sita Devi: '*Ye cartoon tumne banaaya?*' [Did you draw this cartoon?].

Preetam: '*Ji haan*' [Yes].

Sita Devi: '*Ye main aur Anita hain*?' [Is this Anita and me?].

Preetam: '*Ji haan.*'

Sita Devi: '*Aisi shakalen hain hum donon ki*?' [Is this what we look like?].

Preetam: '*Ji haan.*'

Sita Devi: '*Mazaak uraaya hai tumne hamaara?*' [So you mock us, do you?].

Preetam: '*Ji haan.*'

Each '*Ji haan*' has a different shade, a different tonality, meaning different things. I thought, 'Let's repeat the same word, it will thrill the audience.' So the whole scene was evolved in this way. When Preetam said 'Yes' for the third or fourth time, the audience in the cinema hall burst out laughing. The audience loved it. At the very end of the scene, the hero finally responds to Sita Devi's exasperated comment:

Sita Devi: '*Tum is kaabil nahin ho ke koi shareef insaan tumse baat kare. Ab mera vakeel tumse adaalat men baat karega*' [You're not worthy of being addressed by any decent person. From now on my lawyer will do the talking — in court].

Preetam: '*kya aapke vakeel saahib shareef nahin hain*?' [So isn't your lawyer decent ?].

The dialogues of the film are so unlike the predictable lines spoken in most Indian films, that audiences in the fifties, as well as more recent viewers, marvelled at the film's wit and imagination. Each exchange demands complete attention, and unlike many Indian screenplays in which dialogues repetitively stress the same emotions again and again, each sentence in *Mr & Mrs 55* skilfully develops the plot while the dialogue as a whole invokes a range of feelings. A fifties critic wrote,

> Guru Dutt's production *Mr & Mrs 55* premiered in Bombay on April 29, 1955 at the Swastik cinema. A thoroughly delightful, honey-and-cream social comedy. *Mr & Mrs 55* is a model of film craft and has gripping interest for every class of cinegoer. Its satire on characters we know and its incidents taken from life are spiced with humour...the dialogue, well written, tense and witty, enhances the appeal of this true-to-life and thought-provoking entertainer. [*Filmfare*, May 27 1955.]

Another original feature in the writing style developed by Abrar Alvi and Guru Dutt is the way in which they diffuse highly charged situations with witty repartees that are matter-of-fact and down-to-earth. In the convention of Indian cinema, dramatic effect in dialogue is often achieved by accentuating simple realities. Simple questions, like 'How did you get here?' are used to evoke answers with an exaggerated melodramatic tone. Abrar Alvi, on the other hand, made a scene witty through a subtle mocking of the conventions of Hindi film dialogue by providing the most obvious responses to the most banal questions. A question on the lines of, 'How did you get here?' would provoke laughter in the audience by the simplicity of its response: 'By taxi.'

In Guru Dutt's films, Johnny Walker nearly always had the best comic lines, and always had the best comic songs. Even Mohammed Rafi's inflections in the singing of *Jaane kahaan mera jigar gaya ji* (I don't know where my heart has fled to) in *Mr & Mrs 55* are perfectly suited to Johnny's screen persona: a man who lives by a certain folk-intelligence, who despite his perpetual grumbling is always a loyal friend to the hero of the story.

JOHNNY WALKER: In those days, most of the shooting was done indoors, and mostly at night-time. Many of the studios were in the middle of the city, so you'd hear a lot of noise — the traffic, car horns and crows and what-not. It was so noisy, we'd keep having to cut the shot. We didn't do much dubbing in those days, and because we needed as much quiet as possible, we would shoot at nights, from nine in the evening to five in the morning. The atmosphere on the sets was so wonderful that we never knew where the night went. We would be at the studio whether we were needed or not. Whether it was a light scene or a serious scene, Guru Dutt made sure it went well. I wasn't very good at dubbing: they used to have to tie me down to make me dub. I couldn't get the same quality that you get by doing the scene on the spot. Guru Dutt would always try to shoot the scene with synch sound because there was a great difference between dubbing and performing in synch sound. He never compromised on quality, no matter how much extra it cost.

Guru Dutt gave all his artists a lot of room. He wanted us all to give our best. If we made a mistake, then he'd tell us. That's how he was with all artists, and with me too. He used to tell me, *'Johnny, ye tumhaara scene hai, ye dialogue hai, ye shot hai. Isme tum jo behtar kar sakte ho to karo'* [Here's your scene, your dialogue, this is the shot. If you can do better, go ahead]. That's what he would say, then off I'd go. In each rehearsal, I'd say some lines extempore. In every rehearsal I would come up with something new. Guru Dutt used to love that. He used to look at everyone on the set, and see if the light-boys, the cameraman, the assistants, were laughing at my dialogues. Guru Dutt had an assistant to write down whatever I said in the rehearsals. That's how we worked. The reason why I did so well in all of Guru Dutt's films was that I had found the man who knew how to draw out my talent, otherwise it would have stayed within me.

S. Guruswamy recalls how much Guru Dutt enjoyed working with Johnny Walker and how he gave him complete freedom. They were not only colleagues but also good friends in their personal lives, frequently going on hunting and fishing expeditions together along with Abrar Alvi. Guruswamy described how the whole mood on the set would change when Johnny Walker arrived, and smilingly admitted how Murthy used to get annoyed because he found it difficult to concentrate when Johnny was in full flight. Guruswamy added that an amused Guru Dutt would tell Murthy, *'Karne do na, kaahe ko chillaate ho?'* (Let him carry on, why must you yell?).

Guru Dutt was otherwise said to be intolerant of any disturbances on his set. His colleagues remember his short temper, and the many fights that would immediately be followed by a telephone call from Guru Dutt apologizing for being impatient. He bore no malice against anyone but held people to their word, preferring to be told that something was not possible rather than to be given false promises. His colleagues on the set remember his indecisiveness, which was followed by a continuous flow of inspiration. V.K. Murthy recalls one such occasion during the filming of *Mr & Mrs 55*, when Guru Dutt was to film Madhubala as she sings the delightful song, *Thandi hawa kaali ghata* (The cool breeze, the black clouds) on location at a Bombay swimming pool. The Mahatma Gandhi swimming pool at Shivaji Park in Bombay is still used occasionally as a film location, with the blue of the sky reflected in the pool water, the tall palm trees and the pale green tiles lining the pool. None of the surrounding colour is in *Mr & Mrs 55*, but each of those black-and-white images of umbrellas and smiling faces exudes more life than the living reality of an otherwise bland setting.

V.K.MURTHY: Guru Dutt decided to picturize the song at a swimming pool. So we went together with full crew, camera and everything. Then he took his view-finder to find out an angle. How to start the song: to find the very first shot of the song. He went on looking through the view-finder, from all corners of the swimming pool, but he wasn't satisfied. Then he decided, 'I don't think I'll be able to find an angle today, just pack up.' That's all. We packed up. No shooting on that day. Next morning we went there again. The very first angle that he saw through the view-finder, he said, 'Ah! This is it. We put the camera here.' Play-back, one rehearsal, and the shot was set. That's how we started, and the filming of the song continued without any difficulty. It was always difficult for him to find the very first shot of a scene, how to start. He used to go on rehearsing with people. 'People' means mostly myself, I used to take the place of the artists, and he would look through the camera. He was a wonderful person. Very simple, actually he never had any sort of ego, he never thought himself to be a big director, a big personality. He used to mix with all sorts of people. He didn't mind sitting with a light-boy to eat. He used to sit with the workers, talk to them and eat with them. In fact, he particularly liked the food eaten by workers. He never liked wearing expensive or flashy clothes. Never. He was a very simple man, a very pleasant man, but on the sets he was a tiger.

S. Guruswamy remembered the *Thandi hawa* incident as clearly as V.K. Murthy, and added that when they did return to the Mahatma Gandhi swimming pool, Guru Dutt completed the entire song in two days. Guruswamy clicked his fingers saying,'*Phat, phat, phat*, in two days he finished the song. But deciding what was to be the first shot in a sequence, fixing the shot, he would take time. As soon as that was done, the rest of the sequence would just unfold as though it were pre-written.'

A friend from London, S.N. Gourisaria, remembers how particular Guru Dutt was about money matters. He had once borrowed some money from Gourisaria and the very day that Gourisaria arrived at Bombay airport, he was met by Guru Dutt who insisted on returning the money immediately. Guru Dutt was also particular in the way he ran his company.

S.GURUSWAMY: Guru Dutt did not like black market dealings. He found a way to save tax without getting involved with black money payments to artists. For instance, an artist's fee is 3 lakhs. Guru Dutt would pay the artist Rs 50,000 during the making of the film, and the balance of two and half lakhs would become payable in ten annual instalments of Rs 25,000 each. Guru Dutt would place the balance of two and half lakhs in the LIC (Life Insurance Company) in the name of the artist. This was accepted by the tax authorities. The government could use the money, and every year the artist would receive Rs 25,000 and pay tax on it. Many artists have adopted this procedure and are now being paid in the same way.

Though *Aar Paar* and *Mr & Mrs 55* are often categorized as Guru Dutt's two comedies, the films have little in common. If they seem at all similar, this may be attributable to the fact that O.P. Nayyar repeats much of *Aar Paar*'s background music to accompany the action in *Mr & Mrs 55*. Each of Guru Dutt's earlier works has some unusual or memorable moments, but the overall effect of those works — *Baazi*, *Jaal*, *Baaz* and *Aar Paar* — is uneven. *Mr & Mrs 55* is the first film in which a lyrical and poetic style so uniquely Guru Dutt's is discernible. Fluid camera movements, long tracking shots, brilliant use of close-ups, play between light and shade, intelligent dialogue, unpredictable plots, fine use of music, naturalistic performances and a psychological depth to his characters are the hallmarks of Guru Dutt's work. Each of these elements is present in this sparkling comedy.

Although the fluency of images shows a great ease, Guru Dutt was never confident of his own screen presence, and in the initial casting of *Mr & Mrs 55* he had, as Guruswamy remembered, imagined Sunil Dutt in the role of Preetam. But at the last moment, as happened each time a new film was launched, Guru Dutt decided to take the role himself. Preetam is quite unlike Guru Dutt's earlier heroes. Madan (*Baazi*), Tony (*Jaal*), and even Kalu Birju (*Aar Paar*), are recognizably archetypes of Hindi cinema, while Preetam belongs to the real world in which he must struggle to survive. But the humour in the film lightens the very real poverty he endures. When Anita finds him asleep and hungry on a park bench, her own upbringing and naivety blinds her from recognizing his predicament. Preetam tells her that even if he did feel the pang of hunger, there was no bread to be found. She wisely suggests that he might eat cake or biscuits instead. Preetam's old raincoat and worn hat seem his only possessions, and on the day of his marriage he has to 'borrow' Johnny's suit.

The first scene in which we see Preetam shows him asleep — like Chaplin's tramp figure — under a row of stands at a tennis court. Despite her aunt's instructions, the rich and spoilt Anita has sneaked off to a tennis match in the hope of seeing a tennis player whom she mistakenly believes she loves. While escaping her aunt's spy, who has arrived at the match, Anita slips through the row of stands and literally falls on the dozing Preetam. He is so stunned by her beauty that he does not speak at all during the entire sequence of their encounter. Anita rushes away as mysteriously as she has entered Preetam's world. The sequence closes with the camera tracking towards Preetam as he looks longingly after her. In the next scene Preetam, who has still not uttered a word, meets Johnny in a restaurant. Johnny, an incessant talker, demands to know what's wrong with Preetam and why he will not speak:

Johnny: *Abe kya ho gaya hai* (What's wrong with you?).
Preetam responds at last; not in speech, but in song:

Aji dil pe hua aisa jaadu,
tabiyat machal machal gayi;
nazaren jo milin kya kisi se
ke halat badal badal gayi.

(My heart was struck by such magic,
My state of mind's disturbed,
The moment my eyes met another's
I felt myself transformed.)

In Guru Dutt's world the romantic, when faced with obstacles, can only retreat. Preetam plans to leave Bombay, the 'city of merchants', for Delhi, the 'city of kings.' Anita saves the day by escaping from her aunt, and rushes to the airport only to see the plane for Delhi already in mid-air. She is silent with sorrow as a distant song — like a voice in her heart — blends with the sounds of planes landing and departing: *Preetam, aan milo* (Preetam, come to me). True to the world of dreams, Preetam, who was, after all, booked on a later flight, stands before her.

Madhubala was a perfect choice for the role of Anita. She was a far bigger star than Guru Dutt, having begun her career as a child actress. She had also acted in many important Bombay Talkies films, including Amiya Chakravarty's *Basant* (1946). Her first lead role was opposite the then newcomer Raj Kapoor in Kidar Sharma's *Neel Kamal* (1946). This film was followed by many other successes, the most important of which was Kamal Amrohi's *Mahal* (1949). Though Madhubala was to some extent typecast in romantic roles, her natural instinct for comedy enhances the vibrant energy of *Mr & Mrs 55*.

S.GURUSWAMY: When I went to tell Madhubala that Guru Dutt wanted her to act in *Mr & Mrs 55*, she was very happy. Her father was a very dear friend of mine. When they first came to Bombay, I gave them a place to stay. Everyone was very surprised when they found Madhubala so cooperative; they thought that she would be a lot of trouble. In those days, she never worked beyond 6.30 p.m. But she was never difficult with us, she was very cooperative. She was such a nice person. You know, sometimes you come across such people who are over-nice to you, then you feel bad.

Mr & Mrs 55 was a beautiful picture. I had the feeling that Guru Dutt was much ahead of his times. The film was such a beautiful idea. You could never feel tired working on such a film. It goes on sliding, and then you find the picture is complete. Whereas, you take a subject like *Sahib Bibi aur Ghulam*, it affects the mood of the entire unit.

Mr & Mrs 55 is a film full of ideas and shows Guru Dutt's sophisticated handling of comedy. A fine example of its humour is the scene in which Preetam is given a cinema ticket and is asked to hand over a letter to the girl who will be sitting next to him. In the darkened cinema hall, Preetam naturally tries to give the letter to his immediate neighbour. The woman is outraged at this stranger's advances and turns to her husband to complain. The husband glares at Preetam who is saved by Anita's arrival. Preetam then proceeds to give her the letter, and when Anita reads that the tennis player she's infatuated with is leaving India, she bursts out crying. The neighbour and her husband are now convinced that Preetam is some sort of pervert and ask Anita, 'Was he trying to give you a letter too? ' Before the tearful Anita can reply, all the spectators join in to admonish Preetam. Another wonderful and subtle moment in the film shows Anita, who is being forcibly kept apart from Preetam by her aunt, lying on the carpet in her room listening to the radio. The song playing happens to be *Preetam aan milo* (Beloved, come to me). Her aunt, hearing the words of the song, turns off the radio promptly. The next shot cuts to the same song playing simultaneously on the radio in Preetam and Johnny's room as Preetam is packing his bags to leave for Delhi.

Preetam is the first of Guru Dutt's struggling artists. Like Vijay in *Pyaasa* and Suresh Sinha in *Kaagaz ke Phool*, he is an introverted man who is revolted by false social values and inequalities but is unable to take the world head-on. While Vijay uses poetry as his sword, Preetam's revolt is expressed through cartoons. Preetam is the lighter side of Guru Dutt's screen characters; yet he too, prefers withdrawal to confrontation. When he feels that Anita does not love him, he helps bring about the divorce by providing Sita Devi with false evidence of his own debauchery. He walks away from Sita Devi's house as the doors close on him. He walks onto the street, where some street singers are performing a *qawali:*

Karavaan dil ka loota baitha houn manzil ke qareeb,
main ne khud kishti dubo di jaa ke saahil ke qareeb...
kya main karta...kya main karta...
mai sharaab-e ishq se madhosh tha.

(As I neared my destination, I robbed my heart of its desire;
As I neared the shore, I sank the boat with my own hands.
What else could I have done? What else? —
Intoxicated as I was with the wine of love.)

Preetam stands in the half-light so prevalent in Guru Dutt's later work, and smiles in ironic complicity as the *qawal* sings. The scene bears a new intensity not explored in the earlier scenes of *Mr & Mrs 55*. Despite the prevailing light-hearted and breezy tone of this comedy, the bitter-sweet lyric of this song brings a significant shift of perspective to the film, and anticipates the very much darker mood of Guru Dutt's masterpiece, *Pyaasa*.

CHAPTER EIGHT

C.I.D.

On a visit to Hyderabad with Guruswamy in 1955, Guru Dutt was invited to attend a silver jubilee celebrating a twenty-five week run of the Telugu film *Rojulu Marayi* (Times have changed, 1955), in which a young actress named Waheeda Rehman had a small role. The highlight of the film was said to be Waheeda's dance, and Guru Dutt too was impressed and asked to meet her. Some months later he offered her a contract with his company. Waheeda Rehman was born near Madras in 1938 into an orthodox Muslim family. She had always wanted to be a dancer and an actress and when she was ten years old, she started training in Bharat Natyam. Three years later, she was performing on the stage. Her father, a municipal commissioner, died in 1951 when she was still a young teenager. By the time she was sixteen, she had begun dancing in Telugu films.

Waheeda does not believe in living in the past and is content with her present life. She acts occasionally in 'mother' roles but prefers the peace and quiet of her Bangalore home which she shares with her children and husband, businessman Shashi Rekhi, whom she married in 1974. Shashi Rekhi himself once dreamed of making a career in films under the screen-name Kawaljeet, and had acted in the lead role in Mehboob Khan's *Son of India* (1962). Waheeda Rehman retains her beauty and charm. She laughs with great spontaneity, even at herself. It is probably because Guru Dutt's films, starting with *Pyaasa,* seemed to reflect his own emotional life, that curiosity about his relationship with Waheeda has intensified rather than diminished over the years. Guru Dutt reveals his feelings towards Waheeda in the way that he films her: his images leave few questions unanswered.

WAHEEDA REHMAN: I had begun working in Telugu films. I met Guru Dutt in Hyderabad when he came to see my first film. He heard my name was Waheeda Rehman, and asked the distributor of the film, 'Is she a Muslim — does she speak Urdu? ' The distributor told him that I did speak Urdu and Guru Dutt asked to meet me. When I first met him, I didn't think he was a famous and great director because he spoke very little. He asked me a few questions, and I assumed that all he wanted to know was whether I spoke Urdu correctly. The meeting lasted for about half an hour, and then I returned with my family to Madras. I didn't think for a moment that he wanted me to work in his films. Three months later, he sent a friend, Manubhai Patel, to ask me to come to Bombay for a screen test. I was delighted because I had always wanted to work in Hindi films. I met Guru Dutt in his office in Famous Cine Building in June 1955. He gave me a screen test and said, 'You'll have a three-year contract.' *C.I.D.* was the first film to be made; Raj Khosla was directing it. When *C.I.D.* was half completed, the shooting of *Pyaasa* began. Both films were shot at Kardar Studios, and we went to Calcutta for the outdoor shooting. But *C.I.D.* was released first, then came *Pyaasa*.

Guru Dutt gave his close friend, Raj Khosla, the chance to direct a film through his company now known as 'Guru Dutt Films Private Ltd.' Raj Khosla had already made a first film, *Milap*, in 1955 for *Jaal*'s producer, T.R. Fatehchand, but was more accustomed to working as Guru Dutt's assistant than as a director in his own right. On the first day of *Milap*'s shooting on March 8, 1954, when Murthy told him that the shot was ready, Khosla out of force of habit said, '*Guru Dutt ko bulao*' (Call Guru Dutt). Actor K.N. Singh, waiting for the shooting to begin, burst out laughing. *C.I.D.*, released on August 17, 1956 in Bombay, is a crime thriller involving Shekhar (Dev Anand), a Criminal Investigation Department officer who is framed for the murder of a prisoner. Dev Anand and Shakila starred in the lead roles, and Waheeda Rehman was introduced in the film in the role of a good-hearted vamp.

RAJ KHOSLA: Guru Dutt said, 'Raj, make a film for me.' I said, 'Fine', and then I told him about the plot. He said that the title itself would be a hit. He never interfered with my work, he came on the first day of the shooting, but not after that. I used O.P. Nayyar as music director because I was very impressed with his song, *Preetam aan milo*. O.P. Nayyar had composed a flood of hits in *Aar Paar* and *Mr & Mrs 55*, and the songs did well even in *C.I.D.* I'm known for my song picturizations. It's Guru Dutt's skill that I learnt: the use of the face, the eyes more present than body movements. And the use of close-ups — they tell the main story.

C.I.D. brought in a lot of money. It earned 30 lakhs, which is equal to three crores today. Guru Dutt didn't care for money. He was a tremendously generous person. One day, he called me and handed over the keys of a Dodge convertible. I asked him what it was all about and he said, 'It's a present for having made *C.I.D.*.' I remember when the film was released in Calcutta. There were heavy rains and all the flights were cancelled, so we went by train. The journey took forty-six hours in those days. We got thoroughly bored with each other. Finally, when we got off the train, the Calcutta distributor came towards us with garlands and said, 'The film is a hit.' Guru Dutt was naturally very apprehensive as we went to the theatre. He saw the film for only twenty minutes and said, 'Come on, Raj, let's go. You've made a super film, let's celebrate.' This was around 10 p.m. The next morning I couldn't find him in his hotel suite. I went looking for him everywhere, and there he was lying fast asleep in the bathtub, fully dressed, bow tie and all. We had been drinking all night. He was very sweet.

C.I.D. was a major success for Guru Dutt's company and its songs still remain popular, a particular favourite being Geeta Dutt's *Jaata kahan hai deewane* (Where are you going, you crazed one?). This song was edited out of the released film because the censors did not approve of the sequence (perhaps because it showed the police officer in a bad light). Another favourite song in the film is the duet, *Leke pehela pehela pyar* (With my very first love), sung by Mohammed Rafi and Shamshad Begum. Shamshad Begum had begun her singing career in the early 1940s and was considered *the* leading female singer of the screen at the time. By the late 1950s, Shamshad Begum's popularity had decreased though Guru Dutt often chose her to sing for the more traditional or folk characters such as the street singer in *C.I.D.* and *Aar Paar*. Shamshad Begum, now retired, lives with her daughter and family in Bombay.

SHAMSHAD BEGUM: I liked Guru Dutt very much. He was a very good man, a competent man, very human. If you see his films, you'll find that each one is better than the other. I sang for *C.I.D.* and *Aar Paar*. He used to explain what his characters were doing and whether the song should be happy or sad. He'd describe the kind of expression his characters would have, and we'd sing the song accordingly. I had met him when he was an assistant director. He never changed.

Guru Dutt had wanted Raj Khosla to direct another film for him, but Khosla turned down the offer, preferring to go his own way. He said to

Guru Dutt, 'I am a small plant, and I can't grow under a big tree.' Guru Dutt assured Khosla he could return any time he wanted to work with him again. Guru Dutt's gentle instruction did not go unheard and Raj Khosla became a leading director of Hindi cinema and worked particularly well with actors.

RAJ KHOSLA: Guru Dutt told me that eighty percent of acting is done with the eyes of the actor, and twenty percent the rest. It's true, when you look at a person, you look into the eyes of the person. The eyes are the most expressive part. He knew it without being taught. When Guru Dutt was performing in front of the camera, he was always worried that he did not have the brilliance of projecting an expression in his eyes. He used to wear glasses, but not when acting. It was a problem for him to look natural without his glasses, but he surmounted that by working hard on his eyes: how to express himself.

His interest in details was tremendous. If you look out for the details, the details will look after the subject. It's the details that matter. If he was filming a crowd scene, he would instruct each person on what to do or say. He was very careful about the details, that's why his characters came alive. It wasn't just what an actor would be saying or doing that worried Guru Dutt, but what the actor was thinking at that moment in the story.

Although Guru Dutt had not planned to make *Sailaab* (The Flood), a film produced by Geeta Dutt's brother, Mukul Roy, he was persuaded to complete it when the film's director, Ravindra Dave, left half-way through the production. *Sailaab* starred Geeta Bali and Abhi Bhattacharya in the lead roles, and was written by Nabendu Ghosh. The story concerns Gautam (Abhi Bhattacharya), a rich young man who journeys to Assam to visit his father's tea plantation. When the plane in which Gautam is travelling has to make a forced landing due to bad weather, he is hurt and suffers from amnesia. He falls in love with Kanchan (Geeta Bali), who returns his love despite being part of a religious community that forbids its disciples to marry. Gautam's father arrives and takes him back to Calcutta. The shock of Gautam's mother's death brings back his memory but makes him forget his promise to Kanchan. Kanchan follows him to the city and discovers that Gautam does not recognize her. She returns to her village deciding to renounce the world and join the community for good. Ultimately, Gautam pieces together his past, and returns to the Assamese village. The lovers are reunited.

Sailaab was released at the Imperial Theatre in Bombay on April 13, 1956, and received damning reviews. *Filmindia* described it as 'a picture for your worst enemy.' *Sailaab* rarely features in any critique of Guru Dutt's work, probably because no print of the film is easily traceable. S.Guruswamy dismissed *Sailaab* by saying, 'It wasn't our production.' No member of Guru Dutt's regular team except for Abrar Alvi, who is credited with Sarshar Sailani for the dialogues, worked on the film. The film was a financial disaster, leaving Geeta Dutt bankrupt and insolvent. Her insolvency meant that she could never hold any shares in Guru Dutt's film company.

On July 10, 1956, Guru Dutt's second son Arun was born in Bombay while Guru Dutt and his family were still living at the Seth Nivas flat on 16th Road, Khar. Shortly after Arun's birth, Guru Dutt bought a large bungalow at 48, Pali Hill in Bandra and moved there with his family. Vasanthi Padukone returned to their Matunga flat, while Atmaram and his wife left for London where they lived between 1957 and 1961. Atmaram worked in Burmah Shell's film department making documentaries for them. Vasanthi Padukone remembers that Guru Dutt bought many pets including dogs, birds, cats, hares and a monkey. He had wanted to start a poultry farm, but as his work increased, he had to abandon the idea. Guru Dutt's second son, Arun, settled in Poona in 1994 with his wife, Kavita, and two children. Now in his late thirties, Arun still remembers his childhood years and his relationship with his father:

> At least, I have one very clear memory — that I was petrified of him. I don't know why. Perhaps because Tarun was always his favourite. Papa's and Tarun's birthdays were on the 9th of July and I was born on the 10th of July. They both celebrated their birthdays on the 9th but I never had a birthday party. Papa was very short-tempered. He was very fond of animals so we had a fish tank. I used to love to put my hand into the fish tank. I remember one day when I did not know that he was at home, I put my hand into the fish tank and grabbed the fish. I turned round and saw him standing behind me and he just shouted, 'Arun! ' The way I ran, I didn't come before him for two or three days after that. This was in the Pali Hill house, I must have been about five years old. I don't remember him talking that much to us. He was very occupied with his work and once we started going to school [St Mary's in Colaba], when we left in the morning, he was asleep and when he returned home at night, we were in bed.

CHAPTER NINE

Pyaasa

Guru Dutt never forgot to acknowledge the people whom he admired, and so *Pyaasa* is dedicated to 'the fond memory of Shri Gyan Mukherjee', with whom he had felt a great affinity. The original story 'Kashmakash' (Conflict) written sometime in 1947/48 was revised with Abrar Alvi's help and given its new title, *Pyaasa* (The Thirsting one). The central character, Vijay, was originally conceived as a painter but in the final script he is a poet. *Pyaasa* was released on February 22, 1957 at the Minerva cinema in Bombay. The premiere was attended by many leading film personalities, some of whom mistakenly believed that the film would not do well because of its serious and sombre mood.

Pyaasa begins with a narrative prelude, a scene showing a young man lying on the grass in a city park observing the splendour of nature. The young man is a poet and composes a verse which we hear in voice-over:

Ye hanste hue phool, ye meheka hua gulshan
Ye rang men aur noor men doobi hui raahen
Ye phoolon ka ras pi ke machalte hue bhanware

(These smiling flowers, this fragrant garden
These paths bathed in light, bathed in colour
The wayward bees drunk with the nectar of the flowers)

The next lines follow the image of a man's foot crushing the bee:

Main doon bhi to kya doon tumhen ai shaukh nazaaron
Le de ke mere paas kuchh ansoon hain kuchh aahein

(What do I have to give you? O glorious nature!
All I have to offer is a few tears, a few sighs)

Vijay's poems are rejected by an established Urdu publisher, who advises him to compose verse on love and not on human suffering. His two brothers (played by Mehmood and Mayadas) sell his poems as waste-paper and happily throw their brother out of the house despite the tearful protests of their mother (Leela Misra). Vijay tries to retrieve his file of poems but is told that a woman has bought it. One night, as the homeless Vijay rests on a park bench, he hears a young woman recite his verse. The prostitute, Gulab (Waheeda Rehman), assumes that he is a client and lures him back to her house. When Gulab discovers that Vijay has no money and is only after his file of poems, she throws him out. As Vijay leaves, a piece of paper falls from his pocket. Gulab matches the hand-written page to the poems that she has bought. She tells her friend Juhi (Kum Kum) that he is the poet whose verse she has found.

One day, as Vijay wanders the streets of Calcutta, he sees a young prosperous looking woman, Meena (Mala Sinha). Seeing her evokes memories of when they were at college together and in love. Another old college friend, Pushpalata (Tun Tun) happens to see Vijay in a park and insists that he attend the college annual reunion. At the reunion, when Vijay sees Meena again, he recites a poem telling of sorrow and resignation. Meena's husband, the publisher Mr Ghosh (Rehman), is present at the gathering. His curiosity is aroused and he asks Vijay to visit him. Vijay discovers that Mr Ghosh is not after all interested in publishing his poems, but accepts the menial job he offers. Vijay is also asked to help serve drinks at a party to be held at Ghosh's residence in honour of the city's leading poets. At the party, Vijay discovers that Meena is Mr Ghosh's wife. A few days later, Meena tries to explain to Vijay why she left him, and admits that she married for security. Mr Ghosh overhears their conversation and angrily dismisses Vijay. Vijay learns from his uncaring brothers that their mother has died. Overwhelmed by sorrow, Vijay takes to drink. Gulab tries to console him but he is suicidal. One night, he heads towards the railway tracks to kill himself. Vijay sees a poor beggar shivering with cold, and gives him his jacket. The beggar follows him and gets caught in the tracks. As the train nears, Vijay tries to save the beggar but it is too late. Vijay's suicide note is found on the beggar's mutilated body, and all assume that Vijay has committed suicide. Grief-stricken, Gulab goes to Mr Ghosh and offers him all her worldly possessions to pay for the publication of Vijay's poetry. The book of poems, *Parchhaiyan* (Shadows), is printed and becomes an instant success.

In the meantime, Vijay is in hospital suffering from shock. When he sees the book of poems, he tells the doctors that he is the book's author. The doctors do not believe him, they assume that he has lost his mind, and lock him into a mental asylum. Mr Ghosh and his friend Shyam (Shyam Kapoor) are called, and they deny Vijay's identity. One day, the head masseur, Abdul Sattar (Johnny Walker), happens to pass by the asylum, and helps his friend Vijay to escape.

The first death anniversary of the poet is commemorated at a grand hall in full attendance. Mr Ghosh, and the others present, shower praise on the dead poet, declaring that if he were alive today, he would be lauded and acclaimed. Vijay sings a moving song decrying the hypocrisy of the world. A riot breaks out in the auditorium and Gulab is injured. Mr Ghosh tries his best to bribe Vijay's brothers and Shyam to have Vijay committed once again. But they refuse, having struck a better deal with the Urdu publisher. Another grand event is organized to celebrate the return of the dead poet. Disgusted by the hypocrisy of his friends and family, Vijay announces that he is not the poet they have come to acclaim. Another riot breaks out, and Abdul Sattar manages to save Vijay again. Meena tries to persuade him to grab the wealth and celebrity on offer, but Vijay refuses. He asks Gulab to go away with him to a place from where he shall not need to go any further.

The first of Guru Dutt's masterpieces, *Pyaasa* is a romantic melodrama set in Calcutta that tells of the thirst for love, the thirst for recognition, and the thirst for spiritual fulfilment. Vijay is an outsider trying to make a place for himself in the society in which he lives. His only possessions are the old pair of trousers he wears and a worn jacket that serves all occasions and has seen better days. He sleeps at nights on park benches and for a much needed meal even offers his services as a coolie. The man who gives him a rupee coin for lifting his parcels comments, 'What have we come to? Now the educated work as coolies.' The irony of this situation is that the rich and portly Babu — a brief cameo appearance by the brilliant Bengali actor Tulsi Chakravorty — has given Vijay a counterfeit coin. Without a home and without a job, despite his social background Vijay shares the predicament of the many thousands who live on the pavements of Calcutta. When he has the chance to claim the place of honour that his poetry has finally awarded him, he renounces the world. Because Vijay has high morals in a world where immorality reigns, he will always remain an outsider. And the prostitute Gulab, who is another kind of outsider, is the only one who can share his life. Unlike the example of many Hindi films in which the hero is a transparent character, Vijay has many facets to his personality that are gradually revealed. His past, seen in a series of flashbacks, evokes a time when he was filled with youthful dreams of love. He cannot nourish these dreams and reality shatters them.

It now seems difficult to believe that *Pyaasa* went through many changes during its making. After having shot and edited three or four reels of the film, Guru Dutt decided that it was not to his satisfaction. He scrapped the edited material and started all over again.

During the making of *Pyaasa*, Guru Dutt's younger brother Devi Dutt was trained under sound recordist Raman before being sent to Calcutta to learn about film distribution at the Rank Organisation. Devi worked briefly in Guru Dutt's own film distribution concern in Calcutta before returning to Bombay to join the production arm of Guru Dutt Films. In the 1960s, Devi Dutt made documentaries and advertising films before producing highly successful features such as *Aakrosh* and *Masoom*. Devi Dutt, who began his career as his brother's assistant, remembers some of the changes Guru Dutt made in *Pyaasa*:

> The end of *Pyaasa* was changed. In the original version, the film ends at the scene [high-angle crane shot with papers flying about the room] where Vijay finishes talking to Meena and leaves. And no one knows where he goes. Later on, we added the last scene that you now see in the film in which Vijay comes to Gulab and asks her to go away with him. He changed the ending because of the way the distributors reacted. They felt the ending was too heavy. The financiers requested, 'Why don't you have a happy ending? ' It now has a sort of happier ending.

The original casting had Madhubala as Meena, and Johnny Walker in the role of Shyam, Vijay's opportunist friend. Shyam proudly states that he goes where the wind blows, implying that he has no principles. *Pyaasa*'s characters always remain true to their nature. In the first scene when we see Shyam, he has just returned from the court where he has been paid to give false testimony. He will do the same when it comes to Vijay's turn: for money, he will deny Vijay's identity. But having shot some scenes with Johnny Walker in this role, Guru Dutt felt that audiences would never accept their favourite comedian in a negative role and so he substituted Shyam Kapoor. When Guru Dutt discovered Waheeda Rehman, he cast her as the compassionate Gulab and Mala Sinha in the role of Meena.

Guru Dutt himself is the very soul of *Pyaasa* and any other actor in his place seems inconceivable, though Guru Dutt himself had wanted to cast Dilip Kumar in the role of the poet. S. Guruswamy remembers that when Dilip Kumar failed to turn up on the first day of the shoot, Guru Dutt decided to take the role himself. Dilip Kumar explained in an interview many years later that he had declined to work in *Pyaasa* because he saw Vijay as another Devdas, a role that Dilip Kumar had played in Bimal Roy's 1955 version of the film *Devdas* (1955). Guru Dutt wisely gave the role of the cold and calculating publisher, Mr Ghosh, to Rehman, his old friend from Prabhat days. Rehman had previously acted in a number of films in the fifties, but had soon found himself cast in secondary parts rather than in lead roles. Rehman's performance in both *Pyaasa* and *Sahib Bibi aur Ghulam* is remarkable. Johnny Walker as Abdul Sattar, a man of the people, is so perfect that Sattar and Johnny seem to be two names of the same person.

In the darker role of Vijay's devious friend, Shyam, Guru Dutt finally cast Shyam Kapoor, his assistant on four films: *Mr & Mrs 55*, *Pyaasa*, *Kaagaz ke Phool* and *Baharen Phir Bhi Aayengi*. In Hindi cinema the name of an actor often inspires the name of the screen character that he or she will play. The most famous example is Raj Kapoor, who in his own films often played a character called Raj or Raju; and in Guru Dutt's films we have already seen Johnny Walker as Johnny in *Mr & Mrs 55*. The distinction between on-screen and off-screen personae is deliberately blurred. In the case of Shyam Kapoor, however, this congruity of the names of role and actor is probably coincidental. In the role of Vijay's greedy brother, his unusual choice was the young Mehmood, who later became a leading comedian of Hindi cinema. Mehmood also acted in Guru Dutt Productions' *C.I.D.* in the role of the villain.

MEHMOOD: My father, Mumtaz Ali, was working in Bombay Talkies as a dance director. I played the role of Madan [Ashok Kumar] as a young child in the film *Kismet* which was directed by Gyan Mukherjee. When I was older, I worked as Gyan Mukherjee's driver while Guru Dutt was working as his chief assistant. Guru Dutt always had a camera hung around his neck. He used to keep on taking photographs. After that time, I did not see him. One day, Guru Dutt happened to see some rushes in which I appeared. He then asked me to play his elder brother in *Pyaasa*. I told him, 'But I'm younger than you!' When Guru Dutt was working, he used to throw everyone off the set. When he himself was acting, he would shoot take after take. He should be in the Guinness Book of Records for giving retakes.

> Guru Dutt had also wanted me to act in a film called 'Chilman' (Curtain), the story of a *qawal*. But he dropped that idea. He was a moody man, a very good-hearted man. Work was God for him. He was a romantic. When he made *Kaagaz ke Phool*, he thought that it was going to be a better film than *Pyaasa*; but it bombed. I have noticed that whenever a film is made on an artist, it does not run. I personally feel that the public do not want to see an artist portrayed in a negative way. Raj Kapoor's *Mera Naam Joker* [1970] also bombed.

Guru Dutt returned to S.D. Burman knowing that only Burman could create the right musical mood for *Pyaasa*. Burman gave the score a flavour of Bengal, and all his song compositions are brilliantly varied and are always appropriate to the characters who perform them. The Latin American mood of Abdul Sattar's song, *Sar jo tera chakaraaye* (If your head reels with pain) has all the necessary beats to accompany, in perfect comic rhythm the head-massage of an unsuspecting client. On the other hand, the songs that are meant to be appreciated for their poetic weight such as *Ye kooche ye neelaam ghar dilkashi ke* (These lanes, the auction-houses of pleasure) or *Ye mehalon, ye takhton, ye taajon ki duniya* (This world of palaces, thrones, and diadems) have almost no orchestration and suggest the mood of a *mushaira* (poetry symposium) in which verse is recited to a gently lilting tune. Another important contribution by S.D. Burman is in the use of an effective background score of the film which helps to create the subtle atmosphere for a number of individual scenes. Meena, for example, like most of the main characters, has her own 'signature tune' — in her case a simple haunting melody played on a harmonica. Whenever Vijay sees Meena, the same tune is repeated, representing the stirring in Vijay for the love he has lost.

S.D. Burman was born in 1900 into a royal family of Comilla, a province on the East Bengal and Tripura border. He started his career as a singer for New Theatres in Calcutta when S. Mukherjee (who had by then joined Filmistan) asked Burman to compose music for them in Bombay. Burman's first Hindi film was Filmistan's *Shikari* in 1946. When Dev Anand created his film company Navketan, Burman was a natural choice as music director. Throughout his career until he died in 1974, S.D. Burman wrote some of the finest film music of almost three decades, and *Pyaasa* always features in a list of films with his greatest compositions. His son Rahul Dev Burman, familiarly known as Pancham, became an important music director in his own right, having trained under Ustad Brijen Biswas and Ali Akbar Khan.

R.D. BURMAN: Even when Guru Dutt did not use my father's music, he used to frequently visit our home. Geeta Dutt was my father's favourite and there was a family feeling between us. Geeta's first hit song, *Mera sundar sapna beet gaya* (My beautiful dream is over) was composed by my father whom she called *chacha* (uncle). Geeta was very famous in her time; she could sing any type of song: soft songs, cabaret songs, aggressive and romantic songs. She had a real female quality to her voice. Anyway, Guru Dutt fell in love with her. I remember their courting. I used to go with them to Khandala and Lonavla on picnics. We had a lot of fun.

My father's music was not recognized immediately. He made a few films; *Shabnam* (1949) was a success. Then came *Baazi*, a big hit. Sahir Ludhianvi wrote the song *Tadbeer se bigdi hui* [in *Baazi*] in the metre of a *ghazal* [a lyrical poem]; it had the weight of a *ghazal*. It was difficult to compose a *ghazal* to fit in a cabaret style. So my father gave the song a western rhythm composed on guitar. He used to love to experiment. Even in *Jaal*, when he wrote the song *Ye raat ye chaandni* he transformed its *ghazal* mood giving it a regular stressed beat. When he sang the tune to Sahir Ludhianvi, Sahir laughed. My father also insisted that Hemant Kumar should sing that song even though everyone had wanted Talat Mahmood to sing it. When the song was recorded by Hemant Kumar, Guru Dutt wanted to re-dub the song in Rafi Sahib's voice. My father said, 'Nothing doing.' During the production of *Jaal*, the song *Ye raat ye chaandni* started growing on everyone, so it stuck.

When Guru Dutt was making *Pyaasa*, I played the harmonica for Meena's tune. I also composed the masseur's song, *Sar jo tera chakaraaye*. Guru Dutt liked that song very much and said he would use me as music director in his next film. The film was called 'Raaz' and it was to be directed by Guru Dutt's assistant, Niranjan. But the film was shelved and the songs that I composed for it ended up instead in Mehmood's first film, *Chhote Nawab* [1961].

For the film's lyrics, which are the essence of *Pyaasa*, Guru Dutt chose the Urdu poet, Sahir Ludhianvi. Sahir's father, Fazal Mohammed, a feudal lord, though married several times, had only one son. Sahir was born in Ludhiana, in the Punjab, on March 8, 1921, and named Abdul Hai. His parents separated after a long court battle; and the young Sahir stood by his mother, Sardar Begum. In the early 1940s, his interest in nationalist politics and poetry began while he was studying Urdu, Persian and philosophy. Sahir took an active part in the freedom struggle and, because of his personal popularity, he held important positions in various student organizations both in Ludhiana and later in Lahore, where he joined the Dayal Singh College. Sahir did not complete his B.A. examinations, instead devoting his time to editing a prestigious literary journal, *Adab-e-Latif*, in Lahore. In 1944, while still a student, Sahir (his pen name means 'magician'), published his first collection of poems titled *Talkhiyan* (Bitterness), which included his famous 'Taj Mahal'. In the poem, Sahir writes of the suffering endured by the humble folk who built this majestic monument. *Talkhiyan* was reprinted with additional poems by Sahir several times over the years. He was also an active member of the Marxist-oriented Progressive Writers Association, an important literary group which had particular influence in Urdu literature circles in the thirties and forties. Sahir was soon accepted among the great poets of the time.

After Partition, in 1948, he lived and worked in Delhi editing the magazines *Shahrah* and *Preetlari*. He moved to Bombay with his friend, the poet Majaz, to look for work as a song writer in films. Majaz gave up within six months but Sahir decided to keep on trying. One of Sahir's poems, *Mohabbat tark ki maine*, from *Talkhiyan* was included in the film *Do Raha* (released in 1952), but it made little difference in advancing Sahir's career as a lyricist. Finally through a friend from Ludhiana, Mohan Sehgal, who shared Guru Dutt's Almora background, Sahir met S.D. Burman in the late forties. It was evident to Burman that Sahir was very skilled in song-writing and Burman asked him to work on A.R. Kardar's film *Naujawan* (1951). Though *Naujawan* is the first of the many films credited to Sahir, *Baazi* was released before *Naujawan*. The songs in *Naujawan* were as popular as those in *Baazi*, with *Kaise bhulaayen thandi hawaaen lehra ke aayen* (How can one forget the cool breeze flowing in waves), sung by Lata Mangeshkar, proving a particular favourite. Burman and Sahir formed a team working on a number of films, including Guru Dutt's *Jaal* and *Pyaasa*.

RAJ KHOSLA: Actually, I was an admirer of Sahir Sahib right from my college days. I had noted one of the poems that he had written during his college days called *Chakle*, and I sang it at college functions. The poem was *Sana khwane taqdis-e-mashriq kahan hain* (Where are the eulogists of Oriental piety?). This was the poem that Guru Dutt later picturized as *Ye kooche ye neelaam ghar dilkashi ke* (These lanes, the auction-houses of pleasure), with its refrain *Jinhen naaz hai Hind par vo kahaan hain*. The language of the refrain was simplified for the film because no one would understand the difficult Urdu of the original. When I sang that song to Guru Dutt, he said, 'Raj, this is it! This is *Pyaasa.*'. In the form of art, Sahir and Guru Dutt were very close, but they were not close personally.

Sahir's poem *Chakle* (Brothels) is a fine example of political comment combined with humanitarian compassion. Guru Dutt's understanding and identification with Sahir's poetry blend at such a deep level that Sahir's words seem to articulate Guru Dutt's own view of the world and experience of tragedy. Sahir's unhappy romances, frequent as they were, set a tragic pattern that recurred throughout his life. Though his name was linked to Amrita Pritam, among others, Sahir never married and lived most of his life with his mother and his sister Anwar. Sahir himself acknowledged the importance of working for Guru Dutt in the development of his song-writing career. In an interview published in *Filmfare* (January 26, 1962), Sahir noted that the problem with Indian films was their preoccupation with form and neglect of content. Commenting on song-writing itself, he said that the writer of film songs must keep in mind the fact that cinema is a mass medium and so must use simple language, and express complex emotions and feelings in an accessible manner. He added that it was Guru Dutt who gave adequate scope to Sahir's poetic talent: 'The success of *Pyaasa* led producers to show willingness to accept literary songs.'

Guru Dutt is remembered for his indecisiveness, his fickle-mindedness, his habit of shooting and re-shooting. Yet the fluency of many scenes in *Pyaasa* show little of such hesitation. Many individual shots in the film transcend their narrative function and become impressionistic images telling of Guru Dutt's lyricism. One such example (intended originally as the last shot of the film) occurs in the penultimate scene: a high-angle shot of Meena standing very still as she watches Vijay leave the room. He has told her that he will never find peace in this world and is going far away. A gust of wind invades the room and papers fly about them like falling leaves. A similar moment occurs when Gulab, having heard that Vijay is dead, sits on her bed staring into space. The window opens and with it a gust of wind causes the pages filled with Vijay's poems to fly all about her. She knows she must do something to preserve his memory. The next scene has Gulab visiting Mr Ghosh's office to ask him to publish Vijay's poems. Such atmospheric scenes suggest a similarity between Guru Dutt's work and that of Orson Welles. V.K. Murthy smiles when asked if they planned in advance each sequence or each shot:

Those scenes were very well conceived, but they were mostly on-the-spot decisions. It's the Indian method of working. We constructed the sets all right, but we conceived the shot on the set. We would both discuss where to place the camera. Guru Dutt had a tendency to do things extempore; because whatever he had planned earlier would be changed. Many things were changed. We worked with a general outline of scenes, no details. We'd go on the set, and if he didn't find it to his liking, he'd say, 'Okay, cancel it.' Or suppose we shot a scene, and he didn't find the effect he wanted, he'd say, 'Scrap it. We'll do it again.' Actually he has redone many scenes, shooting and re-shooting; this is particularly true of the way he worked in *Pyaasa*. Before *Pyaasa*, he would scrap only one or two shots of a film, rather than whole sequences. People appreciate his films today, but they were not the result of quick decisions, or confidence.

In the beginning, the style of shot-taking in Indian cinema was similar to Hollywood action films, most directors believed in mid-shots and long shots. Guru Dutt was the first to use the establishing shot, followed by close-ups. Thereby the expression of the actors is highlighted and the story becomes immediately intimate, more like cinema, less like theatre. He was also the first person to use the long focal-length lenses, such as 75mm and 100mm. This lens is useful for close-ups, it has the effect of creating movement. He was willing to take risks, to introduce new styles.

Guru Dutt was never very confident about his acting and would ask his assistants to comment on his performance after each take. Atmaram recalls how difficult it was for Guru Dutt to be satisfied with himself, because of his perfectionism. Guru Dutt would turn to Abrar Alvi at the end of a take and ask, 'Is it all right?' and when Abrar Alvi nodded slowly in reply, Guru Dutt would shout in an irritated and impatient tone, *'Bolo na, kya galat hua?'* (Tell me, what's gone wrong?).

ABRAR ALVI: I remember how stubborn he became about one particular shot. It is the scene in which Meena (Mala Sinha) comes to see Vijay at her husband's office and tells him that there are other considerations in life beside love and poetry. Vijay answers: 'When did you give me the chance? When a man has responsibilities, he learns to shoulder them.' The dialogue went something like that. It was a dialogue-exchange in one extended take. We started at 9.30 in the morning. Guru Dutt wasn't used to delivering long bits of dialogue, but he became stubborn and said, 'We'll do it.' He was at it until midnight, still trying the same shot. Once he got it right then Mala Sinha, who was fed up by then, started forgetting her lines. Guru Dutt had finished all the raw stock, he even borrowed some and that finished too. That was his determination and doggedness in work.

S.GURUSWAMY: Guru Dutt used to film many retakes. We had put up a set in Kardar Studios [*Pyaasa* was filmed mostly on location in Calcutta and at Kardar Studios, Bombay] for a scene where Meena comes to meet Vijay. Guru Dutt wanted to do the entire scene in a long take. It was quite difficult. So we had finished take number 78 and I went onto the set. He said, 'Pack up. What can I do? It isn't working.' I said, 'So what, nothing wrong, pack up!' So we packed up. Next morning we went back. First take was okay. That's an artist — until he did the whole scene in a single shot, he wasn't happy.

Though Guru Dutt was hard on himself, Waheeda Rehman remembers how helpful he was in directing her in the role of Gulab. One of the most moving scenes in *Pyaasa* is the dialogue between Gulab and Meena. Gulab has come to have Vijay's poems published, and because the poems reveal Vijay's feelings for Meena she wants to buy them for herself alone. The subtext of the scene throws into relief the values of the middle class and of the poor. Meena offers Gulab any price for the poems, reminding Gulab that she sells 'many things' for a price. The high point of the conversation occurs when Meena demands to know how a gentleman such as Vijay could come to know a woman like Gulab, a prostitute and Gulab answers quietly, '*Saubhaagya se*' (through good fortune).

WAHEEDA REHMAN: I didn't know much about acting before *Pyaasa.* I knew about expression because I had learnt dance. All the credit goes to Guru Dutt in the way he built the character of Gulab. He had everything in his mind. I was a newcomer so it was difficult for me to follow the evolution of the character. He used to shoot and re-shoot so many times, the chronological order of the scenes kept changing. Beside being an actor himself, he was very keen on getting good performances out of all of us. He would not okay a shot if just one actor got it right, he'd make sure we all performed to his satisfaction. If we didn't understand something, he would enact the whole scene. Because he understood rhythm and music and he understood the film medium very well, he knew how to get us to act in the right way. If an actor would say they were tired, he'd let them stop for the day and continue the next day. Sometimes, if an actor was in the mood to complete the scene the

> same day, then Guru Dutt would keep shooting until the scene was over regardless of how long it took. No matter how many mistakes an actor made, he'd say, 'There's nothing to worry about. Do it again. Let's retake.' He was never impatient with actors.
>
> I remember the shooting of the song, *Aaj sajan mohe ang lagaa lo* (Hold me in your embrace today, my beloved). The song was filmed in a studio. The hero, Vijay, is standing on the roof terrace. Gulabo wants to go to him, but she's scared, hesitant. She is in love with him. The song is playing in the background. She isn't an ordinary woman, she's a prostitute. Even if she doesn't want to go to him, love pulls her. Sometimes people are drawn to each other despite themselves because the attraction is so great. I couldn't get the right expression for the scene. Guru Dutt tried very hard to explain it to me. He'd say, 'You love this man very much and you're scared. This man is a different sort. Because of your background. Because of who you are you do not dare express your love for him.' I had to express what the song implied, there were no dialogues in the scene and I couldn't get it right. Guru Dutt said, 'Murthy, put the lights off. We'll talk in peace.'
>
> He then said, 'Who do you love the most in your life?' I said, 'My mother and father.' 'Who do you love the very most?' I said, 'My father, because he spoilt me the most.' Then he said, 'He's dead, isn't he?' I said, 'Yes.' 'Imagine if your father were alive. Imagine your father is standing on the terrace. You don't know why you're afraid to go to him, but you are. There is a force pulling you to him. You're dying to go up to him and hug him.' At that point, I really started missing my father. Guru Dutt noticed that my expression had changed. He said, 'Murthy, lights on, roll the camera.'

The telling of such anecdotes underline the difference between the reality involved in the making of a film, and the experience of watching it: Waheeda Rehman's story sadly breaks the illusion of the scene being the most erotic moment of the film, as it is commonly regarded. Geeta Dutt's sensual voice introduces another ambiguity into the song: that between earthly and divine love. The *kirtan* (devotional song) tells of longing and desire, and though we see Baul singers perform the song, its dramatic interest lies in the fact that it voices Gulab's passion. The earthly love that she feels is given a spiritual dimension through the words: for Gulab's love is one of complete devotion. Filled with desire, she goes up the stairs to the terrace where Vijay stands with his back to her, unaware of her presence. Gulab goes near him to lay her head on his shoulder; but she cannot bring herself to touch him. She rushes away. In the last scene of the film, an instrumental version of the same *kirtan* is played as Gulab — overcome with joy and emotion to see Vijay at her doorway — runs down the stairs of her house to embrace him. Gulab and Vijay are at last united. In *Pyaasa*, Guru Dutt shows how well he understood the subtlety of emotions.

Though many have linked Vijay to Devdas, the similarities are limited. Unlike Devdas, who is lost in a world of his own, Vijay is concerned with the world about him. Unlike Devdas, Vijay does not turn to alcohol as a means to escape. Though Vijay is drawn to ending his life, something within him saves him; but Devdas could not be saved. Gulab, on the other hand, has an obvious role model in the golden-hearted prostitute Chandramukhi. Like Chandramukhi, she sacrifices everything she owns in the world for the man she loves. Neither woman dares to assume that her love will ever be returned; both renounce the material world and adopt a near-ascetic lifestyle. Gulab shares with Vijay a greater attraction for the spiritual world than the material one. As the *kirtan* expresses the devotional nature of Gulab's love, Guru Dutt uses the imagery of Christ as an allegory for Vijay's suffering. When Mr Ghosh reads the newspaper item of Vijay's suicide at the breakfast table, Meena is reading an issue of *Life* magazine whose cover illustration shows Christ on the cross. When Vijay appears resurrected, at a ceremony held in commemoration of his life, he is silhouetted by a haloed light in a manner suggestive of the figure of Christ. Though Vijay longs for recognition, it is improbable that his deepest aspirations could ever be met in the material world. His thirst is hardly the sort to be satisfied by publishers and poetry enthusiasts. Like Vijay, Guru Dutt, never found an inner place of healing.

ABRAR ALVI: I believed that Vijay should not leave and go away in the last scene of the film, but that he should stay and fight the system. I told Guru Dutt, 'Wherever Vijay goes he will find the same society, the same values, the same system.' We discussed the scene at length, but I was overruled by Guru Dutt. So I wrote the ending in which Vijay comes to Gulab and tells her to go away with him to a place from where he will not need to go any further. I asked Guru Dutt, 'Where does such a place exist in this world?'. But Guru Dutt put his foot down saying, 'I like it. It's sunset, they walk away into the distance, hand in hand. It will be emotionally satisfying to the audience.'

That was how he thought. As far as Vijay's beliefs and philosophy were concerned, I never believed in such a defeatist attitude. But Guru Dutt liked it. The kind of introverted character of Vijay in

Pyaasa and Suresh in *Kaagaz ke Phool*, that was Guru Dutt. He had shades of Vijay and shades of Suresh. If he hadn't been such an introvert, he'd still be alive today.

Har ek jism ghaayal, har ek rooh pyaasi
Nigaahon men ulfat, dilon men udaasi
Ye duniya hai ya alaam-e bad hawaasi
Ye duniya agar mil bhi jaaye to kya hai
Ye duniya agar mil bhi jaaye to kya hai

(Each body is wounded, each soul filled with thirsting
These glances of longing, these hearts bearing sadness
Is this the world or a realm without sense?
For what shall it profit a man if he gain the world?)

LALITHA LAJMI: I feel that working in films does change a personality, especially the kinds of films that Guru Dutt made. I remember when Guru Dutt was engaged to Geeta we used to go on picnics, fishing. We had a lot of fun together. Then all those picnics and fun that we had came to an end. I always felt that he had very many disturbances within him. Somewhere in *Pyaasa* and *Kaagaz ke Phool* you find these disturbances in flashes. But I think they were tremendous. Even though we were brother and sister, in those days it was not easy to confide in another person. Quite often he used to ring up and tell me, 'Come over, I want to talk to you.' When we went to his home, he never said a word.

CHAPTER TEN

Incomplete Films

Shortly after the release of *Pyaasa*, Guru Dutt had the lead role as a young lawyer in the film *12 O'Clock* (1958), a crime thriller made by Geeta Dutt's brother-in-law, director Pramod Chakravorty, for producer G.P. Sippy. The film was of little consequence in Dutt's career and was soon forgotten. In 1958, Guru Dutt leased a sound stage at Central Studios in Tardeo and worked from there. He had always wanted to make a film in Bengali and so began to work on 'Gouri', casting his wife Geeta in the lead role. The story was based on a 1943 Hindi film of the same name directed by Kidar Sharma. The planning of Guru Dutt's version of 'Gouri' was started at the end of 1957, and the film was to be made in two languages, Bengali and English.

S.GURUSWAMY: 'Gouri' is set in Calcutta and is the story of a successful sculptor who makes Durga idols for the *puja*. His parents force him to marry and he agrees to marry if his sales are good. That year he earns a lot of money. There are four or five other men with him at the market. When they see how well he has done, they force him to drink to celebrate, and insist on going to the red-light area. When they get there, they sort of push him into a room. The room is dark and he hears the sound of sobbing. He sees a girl in the room who lights a lamp; her hair is loose and flowing. He is amazed to see that the girl looks like the Durga idol that he has made. Somehow he gets to know the girl's story. He is moved by her and says, 'Let's get married.' She is shocked and says, 'You'll marry a girl like me?'. He then negotiates with the keeper of the brothel and pays him money to take the girl away. One of his male companions knows what he has done. For some time they lead a happy life, then this fellow starts blackmailing the idol-maker. When his parents learn the truth, they start mistreating the girl. She doesn't want her husband to suffer, so she leaves. He searches for her frantically but cannot find her. Some years pass. He has almost lost his mind: whenever he makes an idol, the girl's face appears. On the eleventh day of the month, he joins the religious procession in which the idols are immersed in the Ganges. Suddenly he sees a dead body being taken to the cremation grounds. He discovers that it is his wife. Then he goes to bathe in the Ganges.

For the filming of 'Gouri', Guru Dutt returned to Calcutta where two scenes were photographed. S.D. Burman composed and recorded two songs for the film which were ultimately used in another film when it became clear that 'Gouri' would be shelved. The relationship between Geeta and Guru Dutt had deteriorated considerably by this time and it became impossible for them to work together. Despite the financial loss incurred, Guru Dutt stopped the production of the film. If 'Gouri' had been completed, it, rather than *Kaagaz ke Phool*, would have been India's first Cinemascope production.

In 1959, in parallel to the making of *Kaagaz ke Phool*, Guru Dutt gave his assistant, Niranjan, a film to direct. Niranjan had assisted Guru Dutt in four films: *Baaz*, *Aar Paar*, *Mr & Mrs 55*, and *Pyaasa*. Niranjan's 'Raaz' was based on *The Woman in White* by Wilkie Collins, and featured Sunil Dutt in the role of a military doctor. The casting of the film had Waheeda Rehman in a double role of two sisters, Kum Kum as the third sister and S. Nazir as their villainous uncle. The publicity booklet of *Kaagaz ke Phool* carries an advertisement for 'Raaz' and *Chaudhvin ka Chand* under the heading, 'Two more box-office smashers in the Guru Dutt tradition — fast progressing.' The production of 'Raaz' was stopped, and was only revived some months later with Guru Dutt replacing Sunil Dutt in the central role. A few scenes of the film were photographed in the beautiful snowy hills of Simla, and two songs were recorded by R.D. Burman. It is said that five or six reels of the film (now untraceable) were shot and edited when Guru Dutt, who was dissatisfied with the film, abandoned it. Raj Khosla later reworked the story of 'Raaz' into the highly successful film, *Woh Kaun Thi* (1964). Actor Mehmood requested Guru Dutt to let R.D. Burman use one of the songs recorded for 'Raaz' in *Chhote Nawab* (1961), which was Burman's first film as music director.

Guru Dutt also shelved another project — an adaptation of the 1939 American film, *Bachelor Mother*, re-titled as 'Professor.' Advertisements for this particular project and *Chaudhvin ka Chand* are featured in the *Pyaasa* booklet. The publicity material reads: 'Guru Dutt Films Private Ltd's Next Presentation PROFESSOR starring Kishore and Waheeda Rehman, produced by Guru Dutt and directed by Shashi Bhushan.' The film is described as being 'the story of a man who was too young to teach...and too old to love.' Guru Dutt had offered the film to Abrar Alvi to direct, but Alvi had declined. Many years later, Abrar Alvi wrote the screenplay of *Professor* when the film was made by producer F.C. Mehra in 1962 with Shammi Kapoor in the lead role.

V.K. Murthy remembers that Guru Dutt had also toyed with the idea of making a film based on a story later inspiring *Bees Saal Baad,* but decided against it. Atmaram remembers that Guru Dutt had paid the Urdu writer Krishen Chander to write a script, but their collaboration never came about. Sometime in 1961, Guru Dutt had shot one scene of a Bengali film, 'Ek Tuku Chhuaa', but that too was abandoned. Guru Dutt had planned for M. Sadiq to direct a film version of Gulshan Nanda's novel *Neel Kamal*, with Biswajit and actress Nanda in the lead roles, but Guru Dutt cancelled the production of the film a day before the shooting was to commence. *Neel Kamal* was later adapted to the screen in a film of the same title made in 1968 by director Ram Maheshwari with Waheeda Rehman and Manoj Kumar. Guru Dutt had also promised Atmaram that he would produce a comedy film, 'Sh, sh sh', for his brother to direct, but after four days of shooting, that project was shelved as well.

ATMARAM: I found it a very unnerving experience then, and was quite disheartened. When I asked for reasons, Guru Dutt murmured that it was because buyers had not turned up or something like that. It was difficult to tell what really went wrong and why Guru Dutt would drop an entire project. Of course, he could be equally ruthless with himself as well. *Pyaasa* had been almost completed, at least one version of it; the unit saw the film and our special effects man, Kishan Malik, criticized it. Guru Dutt took the comments seriously and began to rewrite the script and the film was shot almost completely again. He used to say that the written word cannot convey what the screen does. He had to see the rushes before he went ahead with a film.

Devi Dutt remembers yet another film that Niranjan was to make:

Sometime after *Kaagaz ke Phool*, there was talk of Guru Dutt getting his assistant Niranjan to make a film called 'Moti ki Maasi' with Tanuja and Salim, one of the writers in the Salim-

Javed duo. It was supposed to be a comedy but it never got made because Niranjan had died, he was over-drinking.

Among the many aborted plans, Guru Dutt had also wanted director Vishram Bedekar, with whom he had worked as an assistant in Prabhat, to make a film for his company. That project never materialized. This trial-and-error method of working resulted in Guru Dutt dropping many projects, and though he had lost money in 'Gouri' and 'Raaz' he was unwilling to compromise on quality. Not only would he abandon the completion of a film, he would often consider casting a particular artist and then change his mind.

V.K. MURTHY: There were many occasions when Guru Dutt would sign an artist; he even paid them money, then he realized they were completely wrong for the part. But he didn't have the courage to tell the actors to their face. He'd tell Guruswamy to do the explaining. It happened so often.

ATMARAM: Guru Dutt paid everyone but then suddenly when he was dissatisfied with a writer or artist, he would say, 'Atma, tell them not to come back.' He would never tell them himself. He had asked Bedekar to direct a picture for him so when Bedekar came, he kept calling Guru Dutt 'sir.' Guru Dutt didn't take him in the end because he said, 'Why should he call me, 'sir', I was his assistant. If Bedekar has this attitude, how will he dominate the picture?' Guru Dutt used to react to small things. Mostly he was right with his intuition. He used to try out so many people. He left a lot of bitterness behind sometimes. But he didn't mind; it was only the film that mattered to him. He didn't care about relationships. I am not like that. I have rarely done this sort of thing. I have also never achieved his kind of success.

The repetitive pattern of starting a project only to abandon it when it was under way is not to be explained simply by a quest for perfectionism; it also indicates an increasingly disillusioned and fractured state of mind. Guru Dutt's personal life was in turmoil, and he drank and smoked heavily. Geeta's singing career had begun to decline. Her unhappy married life led to her dependency on alcohol which made matters worse. Before they had married in 1953, Guru Dutt had asked the scholar Pandit Narendra Sharma, a celebrated Hindi poet and lyricist, for personal guidance. Pandit Sharma had once met Guru Dutt at Uday Shankar's India Culture Centre where Sharmaji had also worked. Pandit Sharma did not have any direct connection with Guru Dutt's films, but his affection for Guru Dutt was enormous.

PANDIT NARENDRA SHARMA: I had first met him in Almora. Though he was soft, delicate, unobtrusive — there was nothing loud about him — yet the roots of his talents lay somewhere very deep inside him and he could perceive things keenly. I remember when he came to me with his horoscope and that of Geeta's. Individually they were very lovable, very good people — artistic, sensitive, with a lot of sensibility. Geeta Dutt had sung some of my lyrics and I knew her very well but I knew Guru Dutt a little better. So I was obliged to tell him that theirs would not be a happy marriage. I thought I had to be frank with Guru Dutt and so I told him. He was silent, he didn't enter into a debate as naturally he must have made his own resolve. He married the woman he loved, whatever the consequences. Astrological forecasts must be considered a part of worldly sanity, but artists are insane. Sanity isn't much of an asset for artists.

I saw him less often in later years when he was so busy, and I became a fan of his films. What was remarkable in his films was that he drew from his inner experience which veered round two points: how persons are exploited and how talent can be unjustly exploited by others. He discussed one of the very early drafts of *Kaagaz ke Phool,* and there it was, this same exploitation. His presence was like candlelight: subdued light, but nevertheless light. He managed to have a team who were very loyal to him. That showed that he had the qualities of a leader but that candlelight could be snuffed out.

In 1958, Guru Dutt obtained the copyright licence from Twentieth Century Fox to use Cinemascope in his next production. Though he also shot *Kaagaz ke Phool* (Paper Flowers) simultaneously in 35mm (as not all theatres in India had the right equipment to project the film in Cinemascope), it is evident that the film was conceived in this format.

V.K. MURTHY: Guru Dutt suffered a big financial loss in *Baaz,* and when he started work on *Aar Paar*, he wanted me to shoot the film as quickly as possible. So there was a lot of pressure on me. Guru Dutt used to get a little angry and say, 'Come on, man, be quick. Murthy, what is this? You're wasting time.' One day, just before lunch, I was lighting a shot. I had to make some touches to complete the lighting and he said, 'Nothing doing. We'll take this shot as it is.' He forced me to take the shot. Everybody went out of the studio for lunch. I sat there, weeping like a girl, because I couldn't do what I wanted to. In my mind I had thought I must quit. After fifteen minutes, Guru Dutt came back into the studio as

I was missing from the lunch table. He said, 'Murthy, you know my position. I've lost a lot of money, so that's why I'm forcing you. Don't sit like a girl and start weeping. What is this nonsense? I'll make a picture especially for you. It's the life of a film director. It will have the beautiful atmosphere of studios, so until then please cooperate with me.' That's how he gave me full freedom in *Kaagaz ke Phool*.

CHAPTER ELEVEN

Kaagaz ke Phool

Kaagaz ke Phool, released on October 2, 1959 at the Maratha Mandir and the New Empire in Bombay, begins with a crane shot of an old man entering the gates of a grand film studio (shot on location at Vauhini Studios, Madras). He makes his way to a vacant set and climbs up to the cat-walk. As he looks down on the empty stage, his past unfolds before him: he is Suresh Sinha (Guru Dutt), a successful middle-aged film director who is separated from his socialite wife Bina (Veena). Bina's father, the thoroughly anglicized Sir B.B. Varma (Mahesh Kaul), believes his son-in-law's profession in films to be disreputable. When Sinha visits his daughter, Pammi (Baby Naaz), who is at a Dehra Dun boarding-school, he is informed that he will not be permitted to meet her again. Sinha goes to Delhi to reason with his estranged wife but she refuses to see him. In a Delhi park, Sinha seeks shelter under a tree from the pouring rain where he meets a young woman, Shanti (Waheeda Rehman). Sinha lends his coat to the shivering Shanti who, as Sinha discovers, is quite alone in the world. Sinha returns to Bombay to resume work on the film that he is making called 'Devdas.' Sinha disapproves of the actress whom the producers recommend for the role of the film's heroine Parvati, called 'Paro'. When Shanti comes to Bombay looking for work and visits the studio to return Sinha his coat, she is inadvertently filmed. When Sinha sees the day's rushes with Shanti's fleeting appearance, he offers her the role of Parvati. Shanti's screen test pleases everyone, and Sinha takes on the task of grooming his discovery. Sinha is injured in a car accident and Shanti nurses him back to health. They become increasingly close to one another. Though they never speak of their feelings, it is clear that they are in love. The film press is quick to spread rumours of their alleged affair. Sinha's daughter, the spoilt Pammi, is most upset when she reads that her father is involved with an actress, and rushes to Bombay to persuade Shanti to leave her father alone. Sinha's 'Devdas' is released to an enthusiastic audience and Shanti is acclaimed a star.

Not wanting to come between Sinha and his daughter, Shanti decides to go away to a small village where she becomes a teacher. Meanwhile, Pammi's efforts to reunite her parents are in vain, and a court hearing awards Bina full custody of their daughter. Sinha, having lost both Shanti and Pammi, is overcome by grief and loneliness. He loses all interest in his work and turns to drink. His career flounders, and his house is auctioned. Rocky (Johnny Walker), Bina's sympathetic brother, tells Shanti of Sinha's troubles. Shanti returns to Bombay knowing that Sinha will be given another chance to direct if she agrees to act in the film. But Sinha refuses, seeing her offer as charity. Shanti is nearly deranged with love for Sinha, but he is nowhere to be found. Shanti stays on in Bombay to work in films.

Years pass, and Sinha has become destitute. He looks for work as a film extra in order to buy Pammi a gift for her wedding. Coincidentally, Shanti is the leading star of the film in which he is given a part role of an old man. When Shanti recognizes Sinha beneath his white wig and beard, she rushes after him, but is stopped by a group of fans who crowd around her for autographs. As Sinha looks back to see Shanti, the flashback ends. Sinha is now an old and broken man sitting alone on the cat-walk. The lunch-break is over, and the studio-hands return to the set. They discover a dead man in the director's chair. An old studio employee realizes the dead man is Suresh Sinha, the once famous director.

A reviewer in *Filmindia* (November, 1959) wrote savagely, '*Kaagaz ke Phool* is an utterly undistinguished picture except that it is made in Cinemascope. It is a depressing, incoherent tale boringly told.' Despite a grand premiere held in Delhi and attended by the then Vice-President of India, Dr S. Radhakrishnan, both critics and audiences hastily rejected the film on its release. In some cities, the film ran for only a week. Only years later did *Kaagaz ke Phool* receive the acclaim it deserved and now it enjoys a cult following in India and in other countries such as France, where it was released commercially in the 1980s.

Kaagaz ke Phool is a fine and subtle tribute to the glorious days of the studio era, using its history from about the 1930s to the end of the 1940s as a backdrop. An early shot in the film reveals Sinha leaning from the balcony of a cinema hall where a well-known film of 1937, *Vidyapati*, is playing to a full house: the films that Sinha is seen to make in *Kaagaz ke Phool* are films that have actually existed. The film to which Sinha dedicates all his energies is 'Devdas', a reference to the classic film of 1935. Guru Dutt shows his appreciation of, and perhaps nostalgia for, the special quality of life peculiar to the secluded atmosphere of studios in a wonderful scene in which we see Suresh Sinha arrive at work. Sitting in the back of an open automobile, the bespectacled Sinha is reading what appears to be a script. As his car slowly drives through the lanes of the studio leading to its main office, Sinha is greeted by the many studio workers as they go about their business. Sinha arrives at the studio to find the music director and his musicians ready to play the latest tune. The script-writer too is ready at hand. The scene shows the immense respect directors once commanded, and alludes to a time when the medium of cinema was considered a craft. The decline of the studio era matches the decline in Suresh Sinha's own fortunes. By the end of the forties, the studios had lost out to the freelancing system. Suresh Sinha discovers that stars (and in this case even his own discovery, Shanti) have more power to wield in a cynical and changing industry.

Though audiences were critical of the film at the time of its release, some aspect of the production won unanimous praise: V.K. Murthy's photography won him his first Filmfare award, and M.R. Achrekar won a second Filmfare award for his art direction. V.K. Murthy's imaginative lighting creates much of the atmosphere in *Kaagaz ke Phool*. The photography itself functions as another narrative thread: the moulding of light and shadow, the flow between static and tracking shots and the dramatic use of medium shots and long shots in many of the film's scenes evoke as much emotion as dialogue or music. The feel of the vastness of studio floors, the cameras, the cranes, the cat-walks, the arc lamps — all those things that made up the reality of the great studios — take on a magical texture in *Kaagaz ke Phool*. The film was shot partly in Madras, and partly at the Central Modern Studios and Mehboob Studios in Bombay.

V.K. MURTHY: In the afternoons and sometimes in the morning, the sun rays pour down through the roof of the studio [Mehboob Studios, Bombay] and the sunlight falls somewhere. Due to the dust in the studio, a parallel beam is seen which gives a beautiful effect. Guru Dutt asked me, 'Murthy, can you give me that effect?' I said, 'Yes, if you shoot at a particular time.' He said, 'No, you've got to create it. We're shooting here for ten days. Whenever the solution hits you, we'll shoot that scene.' This effect was required for the last scene of the film, the scene in which the director Suresh

Sinha dies, then later we used the same effect in the song *Waqt ne kiya kya haseen sitam* (Time has inflicted such sweet cruelty). I thought about it for two or three days. If I were to use focus spotlights it would give that effect, but a divergent beam, not a parallel beam, would be created.

On the third day, we were sitting inside the studio having lunch and our make-up man passed outside holding a mirror in his hand. When he passed by, a ray of sunlight reflected by the mirror flashed inside the studio. I thought, 'Why not use a mirror? That's it!' I told the production people to get me two big mirrors, something like a 4 feet by 3 feet mirror. I kept one mirror on the terrace, through that mirror I reflected the light to the inside mirror which was placed on the cat-walk. From the second mirror, I diverted the light to whatever angle I wanted. So that we could see the beam, I used a little bit of dust and smoke. A senior cameraman, Mr Fareedoon Irani [who photographed most of Mehboob Khan's films including *Mother India*, 1957] came on the set and asked, 'What are you doing, Murthy? Are you using the sunlight?' I explained what I was doing. In those days, people had very conventional methods of working and he was completely taken aback. He must have thought I was a fool. A few days later, Mr Irani was the first person to see the rushes. He came and embraced me and said I had done a good job. It was a good idea but I came on it accidentally. In the next issue of *Screen*, a journalist wrote a long article appreciating me.

When *Kaagaz ke Phool* was released, many people accused me of having spoilt the film. They said, 'Your photography is so distracting, all the attention is on the photography rather than on the story.'

Before asking S.D. Burman to write the music of the film, Guru Dutt was rumoured to have considered music director Khayyam. Finally Burman accepted to compose the music for *Kaagaz ke Phool* and his son, R.D. Burman, worked as an assistant. Guru Dutt asked poet Kaifi Azmi to write the film's lyrics as Burman and Sahir Ludhianvi no longer worked with each other after *Pyaasa*. Kaifi Azmi's reputation in theatre and literature has been considerable and his work with IPTA and the Progressive Writers Association (PWA) is much remembered. Azmi, whose real name is Athar Hussain Rizvi, is from Mijwan, a small village near Azamgarh in Uttar Pradesh. In 1945, when the poet was nineteen years old he moved to Bombay where he joined the Communist Party and lived in the Party commune. Kaifi Azmi's wife, Shaukat, who is from Hyderabad, helped to supplement the family income and joined IPTA working with Balraj Sahni, K.A. Abbas, Prem Dhawan and others. In 1949, when the Communist party was banned, Kaifi Azmi went underground. He had no money and no work. Director Shahid Lateef and his wife, writer Ismat Chughtai, who were living in Shivaji Park in Bombay, were well aware of Azmi's financial difficulties and offered him work in films. Though Shailendra was the official lyricist for Shahid Lateef's *Buzdil* (1951), Lateef asked Kaifi Azmi to write for the film as well. Azmi's two songs including *Rote rote gujar gayi raat re,* sung by Lata Mangeshkar, featured in *Buzdil.* Azmi admits that before *Kaagaz ke Phool*, he rarely took films seriously. But the failure of *Kaagaz ke Phool*, and of others which followed, labelled him as unlucky. Azmi struggled hard to survive as a film lyricist, and only when his songs in *Haqeeqat* (1964) became popular, his luck seemed to change.

KAIFI AZMI: I met Guru Dutt when he was making *Kaagaz ke Phool.* Before that, Sahir was writing his songs, and Sahir's songs in *Pyaasa* were excellent. Perhaps there was some conflict between them. Guru Dutt then needed another song-writer so he asked me to write the songs for *Kaagaz ke Phool.* We spent a lot of time together, we became close. I have very good memories of him. What I liked about him was that he was a very hard-working man. This is very rare in the film industry. He used to drink whisky like all good men do. Even after a night long of drinking he was the first to be on the sets, even before the floor boys.

S.D. Burman played him a tune that everyone liked. But there was no situation in the film for the tune. Guru Dutt said we must create a situation. So I started writing. I tried one version, and another. But he didn't like what I wrote. He said, 'I can't help you because I don't have a situation for the song in my film. I think it's best that we leave it for now, and save the tune for another film.' I said, 'Let me try once more, otherwise it will be conceding defeat.' I sat in the office, and turned my back to the others who were talking and faced the wall. I wrote *Waqt ne kiya kya haseen sitam.* Guru Dutt liked it. In this industry once you have written a song, directors don't accept it easily because they think you might write a better one. But Guru Dutt was different, he would like the very first line of a song. He participated actively in the recording of *Waqt ne kiya* which was sung by Geeta. Even when we recorded the song, there was no film situation for it, but it grew out of the song itself, and later he picturized it very well.

Suresh Sinha might have been a famous and successful director, but his worth is seen to hinge on the success of his latest film. *Kaagaz ke*

Phool has shades of the American classic *A Star is Born* (1954), as both films show the rise of one of its characters in parallel with the decline of the other. Guru Dutt's screen personae may be creative but they are never secure, and any success that they may achieve is fleeting and precarious. The very title of the film, 'Paper Flowers', suggests the deceptive and make-believe nature of fame. Guru Dutt condemns the false values that rule the film world, and mocks the fickle-mindedness of audiences. When five reels of *Kaagaz ke Phool* were ready, Guru Dutt had shown it to his family and colleagues in the industry. He hired a projector from Twentieth Century Fox and screened the film in a *shamiana* (marquee) in the garden of his Pali Hill home. Everyone who attended the screening praised what they saw, adding to Guru Dutt's belief that he had in hand a popular film and box-office success. The rejection of *Kaagaz ke Phool* by the audience was all too personal. Even Johnny Walker, in the role of the rich, eccentric and anglicized Rocky (the name is itself an anglicization of Rakesh), did not manage to lessen the film's dark pessimism for audiences.

RAJ KHOSLA: We went for the premiere at Maratha Mandir. We knew the picture had failed because of the reaction of the audiences at the matinee show, the three and six o'clock shows. Now who will face Guru Dutt and tell him. I went to him just before the interval. He was sitting alone quietly in a corner of the theatre. He said, 'Raj, it's a stillborn child.' How much he had worked for that film. And only now it is considered a masterpiece. He never recovered from that hurt. He felt as if the world had suffocated him. He was never the same after that. The financial failure did not bother him, he didn't care two hoots for money. Money was nothing to him. He was hurt because people didn't understand his film. I remember him telling me, 'Raj, I might not have been able to communicate. *Kuchh to baat hui hogi* [Something must have gone wrong]. Why should the audience not understand me? ' He had made a great film. There is a saying, 'How does one play the flute for buffaloes? ' The audience had to be on his level to understand the film. He talked about it once or twice, and after that he never mentioned it again.

Despite the fact that the stars of Indian cinema have always fascinated their audiences, films that demystify the world of cinema hold little appeal for Indian audiences. Comedian Mehmood rightly believes that Indian films that go behind the scenes of filmmaking have generally failed at the box-office (This is not the case in Hollywood where films such as Billy Wilder's *Sunset Boulevard* (1950) and Vincent Minnelli's *The Bad and the Beautiful* (1952) have known great success). Guru Dutt mistakenly believed that the thrill of filmmaking might fascinate audiences as it had fascinated him. He could never have guessed that *Kaagaz ke Phool* would share the same fate as the films made by his doomed hero, Suresh Sinha. The line between the reality of how *Kaagaz ke Phool* was actually received by audiences and the obsession of failure that dominates the film is frighteningly thin.

KAIFI AZMI: *Kaagaz ke Phool* was technically Guru Dutt's best film. I believe it was his best work. But what he wanted to say in the film wasn't clear. His mental state was like that, he wasn't clear. His home life was in great turmoil and so the script kept changing. There were more scenes that were edited out than remained in the completed film. The failure of the film at the box-office did affect him a lot. He lost a lot of confidence. I believe that the song *Dekhi zamaane ki yaari, bichhare sabhi baari baari* [I have seen what friendship the world offers, all have abandoned me, one by one], was Guru Dutt's own story.

The film was popularly believed to tell Guru Dutt's own story: his domestic situation and unhappy marriage, and his involvement with an actress whom he had discovered. The parallels in the life of Suresh Sinha and Guru Dutt assumed a greater logic as many of Sinha's mannerisms and habits revealed aspects of Guru Dutt's own nature and his method of working. One scene has Sinha arrive on location some hours before the shooting is to start as was Guru Dutt's habit. Sinha's inability to break with the past and make a new future also seemed an intrinsic part of Guru Dutt's personality. Something prevented both Suresh Sinha and Guru Dutt from surviving. Guru Dutt's passion for cinema, his love for photography, his compassion for his co-workers, his striving for excellence — all these are reworked in *Kaagaz ke Phool*. The film also shows Guru Dutt's fascination with death as a release from suffering. In *Pyaasa*, Vijay is drawn to end his life but when the moment of death is near, he walks away from the railway tracks. Yet it is through death that he achieves fame and glory; he is given new life, being injured rather than killed by the oncoming train, and his rebirth provides him with a new social identity as a celebrated poet. In *Kaagaz ke Phool*, Suresh Sinha's death is the inevitable result of years of depression, alcoholism, self-denial and symbolic of the end of an era in Indian cinema. The song, *Dekhi zamaane ki yaari, bichhare sabhi baari baari* (I have seen what friendship the world offers, all have abandoned me, one by one) is used at different stages in Sinha's life, chronicling his rise and fall. The irony is that it is Sinha who is drawn to his own destruction, and who is the one who finally abandons the world. By the way that he films his own death, as it were, Guru Dutt imagines a solitary end for a broken man. The sentiments that Suresh Sinha feels in these last moments of his life are described in the second couplet of the song, *Kya leke milen hum duniya se, aansu ke siva kuch paas nahin...* (What have I gained from this world, all I am left with is tears), which echoes in the empty studio. The greatest difference between Sinha and Guru Dutt is the fact that unlike Sinha, Guru Dutt had not known real failure in his own life. His career until that time (1959), had been fairly successful. Some have suggested that Guru Dutt based Sinha on his mentor Gyan Mukherjee who, despite a very successful initial career, went into decline towards the end of his life.

In a 1963 *Filmfare* interview, Guru Dutt comments on the film: 'It was good in patches. It was too slow and it went over the heads of audiences.' After the debacle of *Kaagaz ke Phool*, Guru Dutt refused to sign another film as director, believing that to do so would bring the film bad luck.

CHAPTER TWELVE

Chaudhvin ka Chand

Despite the financial set-back that Guru Dutt suffered in *Kaagaz ke Phool*, he sent V.K. Murthy to Europe in 1960 to learn about colour photography as Guru Dutt had hoped to make a film in colour. Murthy was attached as an observer to the unit of Carl Foreman's *The Guns of Navarone* (1961), a big-budget war film being shot on location in Greece by the celebrated cinematographer Oswald Morris. Morris' team had no idea of Murthy's own experience, and only realized his importance when Guru Dutt sent a telegram to Murthy congratulating him for having won the 1960 Filmfare Award for Best Photography for his work in *Kaagaz ke Phool*.

Guru Dutt was obliged to take his writer Abrar Alvi off the company pay-roll due to lack of funds, and for a short while, Alvi worked in South India. The production of *Chaudhvin ka Chand* was then started and completed within ten months. By the early sixties, any film made in colour fared better at the box-office than those made in black-and-white, but few producers could afford to make colour films because raw stock was expensive and subsequent developing and printing costs were high. An intermediary solution adopted by some producers involved the insertion of one or two colour reels in their films. As a consequence, some black-and-white films of the late fifties and early sixties included a few colour scenes; and given the appeal of film music in India, these scenes were usually elaborate musical numbers. In *Chaudhvin ka Chand*, Guru Dutt also chose to reserve colour photography for the songs in the film. The film was released at the Minerva Cinema in Bombay in June 1960 and despite the fact that the rainy season had started, the film opened to long queues.

The original story of *Chaudhvin ka Chand*, titled 'Jhalak' (A Glimpse), was written by Saghir Usmani who also wrote the dialogues for the film. Guru Dutt had bought the rights to the story some years before and now re-titled it. M. Sadiq was chosen to direct the film with Rehman, Guru Dutt, Waheeda Rehman and Johnny Walker in the lead roles. Mohammed Sadiq had started his career as a story and dialogue writer for producer A.R. Kardar, who gave him a first film to direct in 1943 (*Namaste*, co-directed with S.U. Sunny). Guru Dutt ignored the advice of colleagues who believed that M. Sadiq's career was over. He entrusted Sadiq with the direction of the film but picturized the songs himself. *Chaudhvin ka Chand* (Moon of the Fourteenth day, i.e. Full Moon) is set in Muslim Lucknow and is the story of three friends: the rich Nawab (Rehman), Aslam (Guru Dutt) and Shaida (Johnny Walker). The film opens at a city bazaar where Nawab glimpses a beautiful girl as she lifts her veil for a brief moment and he falls in love with her. He does not know who she is but finds a torn piece of her veil. At a party held by Nawab's sister, Nawab asks his servant Naseeban (Tun Tun) to find the owner of the veil among his sister's many female guests. Not realizing that the party guests have exchanged their veils in play, Naseeban identifies the wrong girl. While Nawab hopes to find the girl of his dreams, his mother is insistent that he marry the daughter of a Muslim priest. Nawab refuses and persuades Aslam to marry her instead. The marriage takes place and when Aslam sees his beautiful wife, Jameela (Waheeda Rehman), he falls in love with her. In the meanwhile, Nawab realizes that he has tracked down the wrong girl, but is ever hopeful of finding the girl that he once glimpsed. One day, Nawab visits Aslam's home and chances upon Jameela. He rushes to his friend to announce that he has at last found the girl that he loves. Aslam deduces that the woman Nawab has seen is his own wife. The tragic irony of the situation compels Aslam to sacrifice his own happiness for his friend. Aslam frequents the chambers of prostitutes in the hope of convincing Jameela that he is unworthy of her. Aslam believes that she will agree to divorce him and marry Nawab, but Jameela's love and loyalty are unshakeable. When Nawab discovers why Aslam is planning to sacrifice his life for the sake of friendship, Nawab swallows a diamond ring and dies.

WAHEEDA REHMAN: When Guru Dutt started *Chaudhvin ka Chand*, he could have directed the film himself, but he thought that because the film had a Muslim setting, it should be directed by a Muslim director. In those days, Sadiq Sahib had a lot of financial problems, and Guru Dutt wanted to help him so he gave him this film to direct. We later heard that Guru Dutt even looked after Sadiq

Sahib's household expenses. Many people told Guru Dutt, 'You're making a mistake. You're a good director, why are you giving this film to a director who has no market value? Sadiq's recent films haven't done well.' Guru Dutt would say: 'That's the wrong attitude. If a person is good, then he is good, whether his films are successful or not.' Guru Dutt really wanted Sadiq Sahib to make *Chaudhvin ka Chand*, and people loved it. Guru Dutt also gave a lot of importance to character roles. Rehman Sahib got a break because of Guru Dutt. He believed that Rehman was a good actor whether he was commercially viable or not.

K. Razdan, Guru Dutt's publicist, suggested Naushad as music director for *Chaudhvin ka Chand*, but Guru Dutt could not afford Naushad's fee, so he engaged music director Ravi on Razdan's recommendation. Ravi worked with lyricist Shakeel Badayuni and the film's songs, particularly the title-song, picturized in colour and showing Aslam serenading the recumbent Jameela, are an important element of its appeal adding to its enormous popularity. It is ironic that although the film is most conventional in story and in treatment, *Chaudhvin ka Chand* became Guru Dutt Films' greatest financial success. The film also happened to be the first of Guru Dutt's films to be entered in an international film festival, held at Moscow in 1962. The film, however, did not fare particularly well with foreign film critics. Attending the Moscow film festival was the second time that Guru Dutt had travelled out of India: in 1960 he had visited London on a short trip, staying with his brother Atmaram.

Guru Dutt had bought a floor in Modern Studios in Andheri and renamed it Guru Dutt Studios. *Chaudhvin ka Chand* was photographed at the studios and on location in Lucknow by Nariman A. Irani as Murthy was away in Europe. Razdan recalls that the celebrations of the Silver Jubilee (twenty-five weeks' run) of *Chaudhvin ka Chand* were held in the compound of Guru Dutt studios, and included a *qawali* performance. Atmaram remembers hearing that Guru Dutt, in his unpredictable and erratic manner, disappeared before the guests could arrive. A guest at the party commented, 'We've come to a wedding, and the groom has vanished.'

S. GURUSWAMY: Guru Dutt didn't want to direct *Chaudhvin ka Chand* because it was a Muslim subject; and he knew very little about Muslim customs. If you get them wrong, the Muslims get very upset, that's why Sadiq Babu was called in. The script had already been written; Guru Dutt had bought the script's rights from Indian National Pictures. We had once wanted to make a film based on the story of a *qawal*, and as that never happened, we took the title intended for that project (*Chaudhvin ka Chand*) and used it for this film. Guru Dutt loved *qawali* and even had a *qawal* living in his house for a while. The idea of a film based on a *qawal*'s story somehow ended up in a 1960 film made by P.L. Santoshi, *Barsaat ki Raat*.

Kaifi Azmi remembers that Guru Dutt had wanted to make a film based on the 1948 Malayalam novel titled *Rantitangazhi* (Two Measures of Rice) by T.S. Pillai:

> Guru Dutt had heard about the theme of a novel written by a writer from Kerala. Guru Dutt had liked it because it was about the freedom struggle. He asked me if I knew the writer. He said, 'You must know him, he belongs to the Communist Party.' I told him that I didn't know the writer personally but he was well-known and I would make some enquiries. I left Guru Dutt at his Andheri studios and came back home to Juhu. Immediately as I entered the house, there was a call from Guru Dutt asking me whether I had done anything about the book. I told him that I had only just returned home. He said, 'That's the problem, you people work very slowly.' Then I think he went to Kerala, bought the rights of the book and drank toddy and returned home. When he read the novel, he realized it was impossible to film because of its political content. The censors would never pass it. So it fell by the wayside. These were the kinds of things Guru Dutt did, impulsively.

When Guru Dutt and Geeta had moved to their Pali Hill home, Guru Dutt's father lived with them, looking after the running of the house, while Vasanthi Padukone stayed on at the Matunga flat with her mother and Guru Dutt's younger brothers Devi and Vijay. His sister, Lalitha, was by now married and lived separately. Atmaram had just returned from England where he and his wife had lived for four years. On January 22, 1961, Shivshankar Padukone died at Guru Dutt's bungalow in Pali Hill; his death was said to be caused by an allergic reaction to an injection of antibiotics. A few members of Shivshankar's family were by his side when he died.

VIJAY PADUKONE: One of those rare cold winters had set in Bombay that January. I was at Matunga when Geeta called a neighbour to inform us that Anna (my father) was unwell. When my mother and I reached Pali Hill, the doctor was already examining my father in his bedroom. None of us was particularly worried about Anna's health and the fact that the doctor was attending him was a matter of routine. That is why Guru Dutt went to work as usual. At around 11.30 a.m. I heard Geeta scream. When I entered the room, I saw Geeta pressing Anna's chest as he was gasping for breath. The doctor nonchalantly said to my mother, 'Mrs Rao [my father was known as Padukone Shivshankar Rao], I think your husband is dying.' We were stunned. Geeta's efforts failed and Anna passed away.

If my memory serves me well, Guru Dutt was with Mehboob Khan in Bandra, so he was the first to come home, followed by Devi, Atma and Lalli [Lalitha]. Everyone was in a daze and there was an eerie silence in the house when suddenly I saw Guru Dutt having a heated argument with the doctor. He angrily asked the doctor to leave at once. My mother did not believe in rituals so I do not remember seeing any priest performing the last rites. Guru Dutt's unit members, we brothers, sister and a handful of relatives performed the rituals, and Anna was cremated that evening at around 6 p.m. When we returned home, Amma instructed everyone to go back to work. But the following day was a Sunday. Guru Dutt went to Lonavla after taking permission from my mother. That was the first death in the Padukone family and Anna's death was too much for us to bear. He was a frail looking man, only sixty-one yet he looked older than his age because of his white beard.

Vasanthi Padukone remembers that Guru Dutt visited Haji Malang Baba's shrine in Kalyan after his father's death as he did whenever he was depressed. Shivshankar Padukone was a reserved and learned man whose talent for writing poetry was never recognized; and though Vasanthi was the dominant force in the family, all the Padukone children were deeply attached to their father. Vijay in *Pyaasa* may have echoed the sense of rejection and frustration as experienced by Guru Dutt's own father. Shivshankar's many poems were never published in his lifetime and now they cannot be found. In a 1963 *Filmfare* interview, Guru Dutt remembered how in his early life he had resented his father's lack of enterprise: '... it was only years later that I realized that worldly success is not so important.'

ATMARAM: My father was a thoroughly impractical man, a simple person who always spoke the truth. He worked all his life as a clerk in a commercial firm (Burmah Shell), and also had an astonishing capacity to write. He wrote poetry and essays in English; he knew no other language except Kannada. Comparing this with my mother's knowledge of several languages, he would always say that he was unable to perfect one language (English) and where was the time for other languages. Guru Dutt acquired my father's sense of perfection and my mother's great abilities, her love for art and her everlasting zest for life.

In parallel with making his own films, Guru Dutt took acting roles in other productions. Of all the films that Guru Dutt starred in for different banners, *Sautela Bhai* is most remembered for his moving performance as the step-brother, Gokul. He showed his professionalism by having his head shaved, since the role required him to be in mourning. During the making of *Sautela Bhai* (released in 1962), directed by Mahesh Kaul and filmed at Guru Dutt's studios in Andheri, he began the production of *Sahib Bibi aur Ghulam.*

CHAPTER THIRTEEN

Sahib Bibi aur Ghulam

After Guru Dutt's father died, a sense of disorder reigned at the family home in Pali Hill. The success of *Chaudhvin ka Chand* allowed Guru Dutt to buy the rights of Bimal Mitra's novel *Sahib Bibi aur Ghulam* that he had probably read in the original Bengali. The novel had already been adapted to the screen in a successful 1956 Bengali version directed by Kartick Chattopadhyay starring Uttam Kumar as Bhoothnath and Sumitra Devi as Chhoti Bahu. Guru Dutt called Abrar Alvi back from South India to work on the new production; and Alvi and Mitra spent two months together in Khandala translating the novel into Hindi-Urdu. Guru Dutt asked Abrar Alvi to tape the entire script in his own voice in Urdu so that he might have a sense of its dramatic interest.

RAJ KHOSLA: I think *Sahib Bibi aur Ghulam* was closest to Guru Dutt's heart. More than *Pyaasa* — *Pyaasa* was his youth, the thoughts of his youth, a story of a young man joining life. *Sahib Bibi aur Ghulam*, on the other hand, was totally mature. It's an immaculate film.

The first scene of the film reveals Bhoothnath (Guru Dutt), a middle-aged architect, wandering through the ruins of an old *haveli* or ancestral mansion. A woman's voice calls him, bringing back his past when as a young, simple, but educated, villager he had come to find work in Calcutta. The flashback begins: it is the end of the nineteenth century and the mansion is at the peak of its splendour. Through Bhoothnath's eyes, the story of the *haveli* unfolds, telling of its owners the Chowdhurys, a family of Bengali zamindars (land-owning gentry).

Bhoothnath lives in the grand *haveli* with its multitude of servants and hangers-on, but works beyond its compound at the Mohini Sindoor factory run by Suvinay Babu (Nazir Hussein). Suvinay Babu is a dedicated member of the Bengali Hindu reformist movement, the

Brahmo Samaj. He has a young daughter, Jabba (Waheeda Rehman) who cannot help but make fun of Bhoothnath whom she regards as an unsophisticated rustic. Bhoothnath becomes fascinated with the goings-on in the *haveli* and its many rooms, and returning home from work every night he observes the decadent life-style of the two Chowdhury brothers Manjhle Babu (Sapru) and Chhote Babu (Rehman). The brothers seldom work but spend most of their waking hours in pigeon-racing or languishing drunkenly in the company of dancer-prostitutes, having happily left their wives to distract themselves by having jewellery made and re-made. One night the servant Bansi (Dhumal) takes Bhoothnath to meet the younger zamindar's wife, Chhoti Bahu (Meena Kumari). Chhoti Bahu implores Bhoothnath to bring her some 'Mohini Sindoor' (bridal vermilion), believing that it will help keep her unfaithful husband home. Bhoothnath is struck by Chhoti Bahu's beauty and sadness and inadvertently becomes her secret confidante. Because of his friendship with Chhoti Bahu, Bhoothnath's confidence grows and soon his beloved Jabba returns his love. One day, a bomb explodes in the market-place and Bhoothnath is injured in the ensuing cross-fire between freedom fighters and British soldiers. Jabba takes care of Bhoothnath until Bansi comes to take him back to the *haveli*, telling him that the 'Mohini Sindoor' has not helped Chhoti Bahu at all.

Chhoti Bahu's repeated attempts to appease her husband have failed until she reluctantly becomes his drinking companion in order to keep him by her side. Bhoothnath becomes a trainee architect and goes away to work on a building project. When he returns to Calcutta some years later, he finds that Suvinay Babu has died and through a strange quirk of fate it is revealed that Jabba and Bhoothnath were betrothed as children.

Bhoothnath returns to the *haveli* and is shocked to find it in partial ruins. Through laziness and a lack of business acumen, the zamindars have signed away their fortune. Their decline is matched by the deteriorated state of Chhoti Bahu and her husband, who has become paralysed. The beautiful Chhoti Bahu, now a desperate alcoholic, asks Bhoothnath to accompany her to a nearby shrine to pray for her ailing husband. Their conversation is overheard by Manjhle Babu, who orders his henchmen to punish his sister-in-law, Chhoti Bahu, for committing the grave crime of consorting with a man, an outsider to the Chowdhury household. Bhoothnath and Chhoti Bahu travel in the carriage. They talk as old friends, and Bhoothnath tells her that he is already married. The carriage stops abruptly in the dark of the night, Bhoothnath is knocked unconscious. When he wakes up in a hospital bed some days later, Bansi is by his side. The old servant tells him that Chhoti Bahu has disappeared and that his Chhote Babu has died. The flashback ends. Bhoothnath's workers inform him that a skeleton has been found buried in the ruins of the *haveli*. When Bhoothnath sees the corpse, he knows from its jewellery that it is Chhoti Bahu's mortal remains.

The film's brilliant performances, rich dialogues and heightened atmosphere make *Sahib Bibi aur Ghulam* a magnificent and sombre work. The film records a period of Bengali history through the lives of the Chowdhurys — a land-owning family who can be seen as archetypes of the privileged zamindar class. A subtext of the film is the inexorable march of time and its power to rule over the fortunes of man. A scene in the film alludes to this underlying theme in which a new order must replace the old order: Bhoothnath strays into a room in the *haveli* where the demented Ghadi Babu is in charge of the mansion clocks. Despite his evident insanity, Ghadi Babu (Harin Chattopadhyay) has that inner vision and wisdom often found in the mad seer, and he alone can predict the end of the zamindari era. He warns Bhoothnath to stay away from these old mansions, these palaces which will be reduced to dust by Time.

The servant Bansi acts as chronicler of the Chowdhurys' history — though protesting, after each of several long and detailed accounts of the goings-on in the household, that *'Ye ghar-ma to humen kaam-kaj ke maare baat karne ki bhi phursat naahin'* (There's so much work in this house that I don't have a moment to talk). Bansi's proud and unquestioning dedication to his master demonstrates the feudal atmosphere of the zamindari *haveli*, and is redolent of an age in which the relationship of master and servant was one of mutual dependence. His character not only adds to the film's historical depth, but also, through his on-screen explanations of events to Bhoothnath, provides the continuity between successive periods in the narrative.

Bansi's function as chronicler is balanced by Bhoothnath's role as witness to the ravages of time and change in the Chowdhury household; the narrative is told largely from his perspective, with other events being relayed by Bansi's reports. Bhoothnath's own history stands in sharp contrast to the social conservatism of the zamindar class: he has emerged from humble rural beginnings, with no privilege beyond his Brahmin status, to become the successful architect who, in one of the film's many ironies, himself oversees the destruction of the zamindari *haveli* which had so overawed him when he first came to the big city in search of work. His very name, 'Bhoothnath' — an epithet of Shiva the Destroyer, suggestive of an archaic traditionalism derided by all the people he encounters except the devout Chhoti Bahu — itself puts him at a remove from the domestic decadence of the zamindars. The particular circumstances of his period of residence in the *haveli* offer him privileged access to an unusual range of different social settings: he works in the commercial world, but also has access not only to the outer part of the family *haveli* where the menfolk live and are entertained by dancing-girls, but also, through his friendship with Chhoti Bahu, to the *zenana* or inner apartments of the Chowdhury women. Bhoothnath's function is to observe the eroding fortunes of the land-owning aristocracy as a new business class rises to prominence.

Even though she appears in less than a third of the film, Chhoti Bahu is the pivotal character of *Sahib Bibi aur Ghulam*; her personality is ambiguous, and is perceived differently by different people. For her obese sister-in-law, Chhoti Bahu is a simple and foolish woman who has not learned to enjoy her new status and wealth. For Bhoothnath, Chhoti Bahu is an ethereal being who is always beyond his reach and in whom he sees both beauty and death: in the first sequence of the film we hear a ghostly voice, that of Chhoti Bahu's, beckoning Bhoothnath into the ruins of what used to be her lavish quarters. The style of this opening scene evokes the genre of the fantastic or the ghost or horror story, and this eerie atmosphere is reinforced when Chhoti Bahu is first introduced within the narrative. She is seen as a spectral figure haunting the rooms and balconies of the *haveli*. Her silhouetted figure looms in the distance as Bhoothnath, having just been woken from his sleep by her song of lament, *Koi door se awaaz de chale aao* (Someone calls from afar, come to me), looks on in a dream-like state.

The build-up to the moment when we first see Chhoti Bahu is reminiscent of Carol Reed's introduction to Harry Lime (Orson Welles) in *The Third Man* (1949), and in a similar manner shows cinema's wonderful ability to mythify its own characters. The entire sequence of Chhoti Bahu's introduction is seen from Bhoothnath's perspective and because he is terrified of meeting her, his eyes are lowered: the camera takes Bhoothnath's angle of view and follows the patterns of a rich carpet on which he walks to enter the room. We hear Chhoti Bahu, still off screen, telling him to be seated. Then we see a pair of feet adorned by *alta* vermilion colour walk across the room; this is as high as Bhoothnath's eyes dare venture. He sits humbly on the floor and is asked his name. Finally when he does look up, the camera tracks in dramatically and holds on a close-up of Chhoti Bahu. Her intense and tragic aura startles Bhoothnath, and from that first look, he becomes forever her slave — her '*ghulam*' as referred to in the film's title.

For her husband, Chhoti Bahu is an ordinary, bland woman from a poor background whose traditional upbringing teaches her to be the perfect wife, and to regard him as a god. When Chhoti Bahu marries and enters the *haveli*, she becomes the property of the Chowdhurys, losing her own identity altogether — in fact she is never called by her own name, not even by her husband, since everyone refers to her by her title as younger daughter-in-law, 'Chhoti Bahu.' Her genuine belief in the sanctity of marriage has no place in her new home, and her husband does not stop short of reminding her that the sexual appetite of Chowdhury men cannot be satisfied by their wives. Chhoti Bahu is not content to be a subservient and docile wife, and fights for her husband's attention, demanding that her own sexual needs be met.

The very fact that Chhoti Bahu articulates her sexual needs puts her ahead of her times. Even in the sixties when *Sahib Bibi aur Ghulam* was released, the heroines of Indian popular cinema, particularly the wives, were never seen to have any sexuality of their own, let alone make sexual demands. The childless Chhoti Bahu even dares to suggest that Chhote Babu is probably impotent despite all his masculine bravura. Chhote Babu is the end of a line, and the family name has no chance of survival. Chhoti Bahu, too, does not escape the decadence of the zamindari era in which she is its final victim. When she ventures out of the *haveli* for the first and only time, it costs her her life. Manjhle Babu, who has lost all his fortune and status, has only his ring to offer his henchmen for killing the innocent Chhoti Bahu. In this last show of power, Manjhle Babu destroys the one person who brought dignity to their decaying world.

Guru Dutt attended one of the first public shows of *Sahib Bibi aur Ghulam* in a Bombay cinema hall, and saw how the audiences reacted to a shot featured in the last song of the film, *Sahil ki taraf kishti le chal* (Steer the boat to the shore), which showed Chhoti Bahu resting her head on Bhoothnath's lap on their fateful and only outing. Devi Dutt, who was working with Guru Dutt at the time, remembers the audience's reaction to the scene:

> Guru Dutt always cared about what the audience felt; he used to send us to see his films in cinema halls and then we would ring him to tell him how the audience reacted. I think the worst was in *Sahib Bibi aur Ghulam*. There were some scenes that the public did

> not like, especially the scene where Bhoothnath and Chhoti Bahu are in the carriage, and she puts her head on his lap. We went to the three o'clock show at the Minerva Cinema [Bombay] and when the scene started, people were laughing and whistling. We called Guru Dutt and asked him to come to the theatre for the next day's matinee show. He arrived just after the interval at around 4.30 p.m. He sat in the balcony and he could see that people were getting restless; they started talking as the film was running. We went immediately to the theatre manager's office and Guru Dutt told us to telephone Meena Kumari to tell her that we have to re-shoot a scene at once. Meenaji was in Lonavla but somehow we persuaded her to be on the set the next day. She had no idea which scene had to be re-shot. In the original film, we do not know what becomes of Chhote Babu so we shot an additional scene with Rehman as well. Then we inserted the new scenes into every print in town.

The bridging scene inserted near the end of the film shows the paralyzed Chhote Babu at last repenting his sinful and decadent ways. Guru Dutt also cut the entire song, *Sahil ki taraf* — which included the offending shot from all the release prints — changing the carriage scene to feature a dialogue exchange between Chhoti Bahu and Bhoothnath. (The tune of *Sahil ki taraf* was re-used by music director Hemant Kumar in the song *Ya dil ki suno duniya valon,* in the 1966 film *Anupama*).

In an article titled 'Classics and Cash', featured in the annual publication of *Celluloid* (1963) and reprinted by Firoze Rangoonwalla in his 1973 monograph, *Guru Dutt,* Guru Dutt has some interesting comments on the audience reaction to *Sahib Bibi aur Ghulam*:

> My decision to take up the novel, *Sahib Bibi aur Ghulam,* for filming was also taken with a pinch of salt by film prophets. Of course, the introduction on the screen of a pious wife taking to liquor-drinking even for the sake of winning over her husband was fraught with great peril. But I took the plunge as at the base of it all was a fascinating novel. I must say the press hailed this attempt with an acclaim which was beyond my expectations. The public reaction was also very encouraging as a whole. In its early screenings at Bombay there was an uproar against only two particular scenes. The first of these was the one in which Chhoti Bahu, out of an affectionate affinity between them, rests her head on the lap of Bhoothnath. The second one was the scene in which she tells her husband, 'Allow me to take the last sip of liquor. Only for the last time. I have decided to give it up completely.' We deleted these scenes.

Sahib Bibi aur Ghulam was a modest commercial success, dividing audiences. The more traditional could not accept that a pious Hindu wife could take to drink; nor could they accept the friendship between Bhoothnath and Chhoti Bahu, given the strict conventions concerning relations between men and women. The review featured in the *Times of India* (June 24, 1962), however, showered much praise on the film and included comments on how effectively the book had been adapted to the screen:

> The well-knit screenplay, achieving an effective balance between the various characters and emotional phases, provides a neat dramatic pattern. It appears to be a specially successful job considering the verbosity and digressiveness of the novel of Mr Bimal Mitra who, though often brilliant, writes in a highly disorderly way. The picture follows the book efficiently rather than faithfully.

In 1962, *Sahib Bibi aur Ghulam* won Filmfare awards in the following four categories: Best Film, Best Director (Abrar Alvi), Best Photography (the second award to V. K. Murthy for a Guru Dutt film), and Best Actress (Meena Kumari, a third-time recipient of the award having first won it in 1952 for *Baiju Bawra*, and then in the consecutive year for *Parineeta*). She had also been nominated Best Actress for two other films in 1962: *Aarti*, and *Main Chup Rahoungi;* but her performance in *Sahib Bibi aur Ghulam* was considered the best of the three.

Guru Dutt, Abrar Alvi and Waheeda Rehman attended the Berlin Film Festival in June 1963 as *Sahib Bibi aur Ghulam* was one of India's entries along with Satyajit Ray's *Mahanagar*. Satyajit Ray and his wife were also present at the festival, and spent an evening together with Guru Dutt at a party held in their honour by the Indian ambassador. It is interesting to compare *Sahib Bibi aur Ghulam* with Satyajit Ray's *Jalsaghar* made in 1956: both films bear a resemblance in their fine observation of this particular period in the history of Bengal, but unlike Ray's dignified and cultured zamindar, the Chowdhurys of *Sahib Bibi aur Ghulam* evoke little sympathy.

ATMARAM: Guru Dutt was always considered a commercial film-maker and whatever reputation he gathered later is something altogether different. But Satyajit Ray had status even in those days; he had won many awards abroad. I believe Guru Dutt met him at the Berlin Film Festival in 1963. Guru Dutt thought highly of Ray. I saw *Pather Panchali* (1955) in its eleventh or twelfth week in a cinema hall in Calcutta. It even celebrated a silver jubilee. Ray was really made by his own people, and an educated audience. Whereas Guru Dutt was a man of the masses. His style was influenced by Barua and the Prabhat films but he was essentially a commercial film-maker.

Meena Kumari was also invited to Berlin with her husband, Kamal Amrohi, but when Amrohi refused the invitation, Meena Kumari, who had never been abroad before that time, decided not to attend. The screening of *Sahib Bibi aur Ghulam* provoked little reaction at the Berlin Film Festival and Guru Dutt soon returned to India. The film was nominated as an Indian entry for the Oscars, but did not win any award in America either. At home, however, *Sahib Bibi aur Ghulam* won further recognition, being given the President's silver medal in 1964, and a 'film of the year' award from the Bengal Film Journalists Association.

As was his usual practice, Guru Dutt had first offered the role of Bhoothnath to another actor, in this case Shashi Kapoor. He also considered actor Biswajit; but at the last minute he changed his mind and decided to take the part himself. Bhoothnath is one of the finest of Guru Dutt's performances; he brings pathos and sensitivity to the character. Rehman was a natural for the role of Chhote Babu which he performs with ease and brilliance. Guru Dutt cast Sapru, a colleague from the Prabhat days, in the role of the elder zamindar, Manjhle Babu. Because Sapru was believed to have an overly theatrical tone in his dialogue delivery, as Manjhle Babu he only speaks once in the entire film. His silence adds effectively in creating a menacing and sinister presence.

Guru Dutt failed to persuade S.D. Burman and Sahir Ludhianvi to work on the film. Burman was unwell and could not work, and Sahir declined the offer. Guru Dutt then chose the Bengali music director Hemant Kumar, who was also a well-established play-back singer, to compose the film's music; and Shakeel Badayuni, a celebrated poet/lyricist to write the songs. Hemant Kumar Mukhopadhyay was born in Benaras in 1920 and from 1937, when he was only seventeen, he began to sing for the radio in Calcutta. He had trained for a short time in classical music but his own preference was Rabindra Sangeet, the music based on the lyrics of Rabindranath Tagore. In 1940, he sang for the first time in a Bengali film, *Nemai Sanyas,* and it was only in 1952 that he began to compose music for Hindi cinema with

Anandmath. His first major success was in the film *Nagin* (1954), and its recordings remained the highest selling for many years.

Hemant Kumar's music gives a haunting quality to *Sahib Bibi aur Ghulam*. The songs are delicate and fine, especially Chhoti Bahu's erotic song of lament, *Na jao saiyyan* (Beloved, do not go), which was based on a Hemant Kumar song in Bengali, *Oliro katha sune*. The film's background score is highly atmospheric. The sadness in Chhoti Bahu is given expression in the melancholic music that is repeated in every scene in which Bhoothnath encounters her. Chhoti Bahu's 'signature tune' adds enormously to the aura of tragedy that surrounds her. Hemant Kumar clearly had a special talent for composing music with an ethereal quality; and it is a score of his that adds much of the ghostly atmosphere in another 1962 release, *Bees Saal Baad*, made by the art director of *Sahib Bibi*, Biren Naug, who worked on other Guru Dutt films.

Guru Dutt had wanted Nargis to act in the film as Chhoti Bahu, but by that time she had virtually retired from films. It was also rumoured that Nargis was not very keen to work with Guru Dutt because her husband, Sunil Dutt, had been dropped from the 'Raaz' project. Guru Dutt briefly considered photographer Jitendra Arya's wife, Chhaya, who was living in London at the time and had never appeared on screen before; but he changed his mind and finally succeeded in persuading Meena Kumari to take the role. Meena Kumari's natural talent for portraying tragic characters brings a unique depth and subtlety to her interpretation of Chhoti Bahu. In Vinod Mehta's biography, *Meena Kumari* (Jaico Publishing House, Bombay 1972), the author comments that he believed Meena Kumari, who was thirty-two at the time of filming, gave her best performance ever in *Sahib Bibi aur Ghulam*. Meena Kumari's personal diary is quoted in Mehta's biography, and describes the obsession that the actress had with her character,

> This woman is troubling me a great deal. All day long — and a good part of the night — it is nothing else but Chhoti Bahu's helplessness, Chhoti Bahu's sorrows, Chhoti Bahu's smiles, Chhoti Bahu's hopes, Chhoti Bahu's tribulations, Chhoti Bahu's endurance, Chhoti Bahu's, Chhoti Bahu's, Chhoti Bahu's ... Oh ! I am sick of it.

Costume designer Bhanu Athaiya who worked on *Sahib Bibi aur Ghulam* and five other Guru Dutt films (*C.I.D.*, *Pyaasa, Kaagaz ke Phool, Chaudhvin ka Chand* and *Baharen Phir Bhi Aayengi*), and whose screen name was Bhanumati, started her career as an illustrator/designer at *Eve's Weekly*. She believed that Guru Dutt trusted her because he knew that she would not design garish clothes. Bhanu Athaiya remembered that Guru Dutt insisted on perfection and gave her plenty of time so that she achieve the desired effect in the film. He also sent Bhanu Athaiya to Calcutta and arranged for her to meet some zamindar families realizing that she did not know enough about Bengal. She was told that she had to create costumes for the film's most important groups: the zamindars, Chhoti Bahu from her modest background and the Brahmo Samajists. There were two main groups of dressmakers in that period who worked for films. The first group, trained in the West, ran boutiques making the kind of fantasy clothes associated with Hollywood extravaganzas; and the second group were Muslim tailors from Uttar Pradesh, who made more traditional clothing. Bhanu Athaiya's preference was for the Muslim tailors, and her costume designs in *Sahib Bibi aur Ghulam* are elegant reminders of a lost age.

The film's art director, Biren Naug, was also remarkably successful in recreating the authenticity of the period whether on set or on location.

V.K. MURTHY: All the interiors of *Sahib Bibi aur Ghulam* were shot in our studio in Bombay [Modern Studios, Andheri], and we filmed the exteriors in a *haveli* about forty miles from Calcutta in a place called Dhankuria. The old *haveli* had forty or fifty rooms and belonged to the Gaine Brothers who were zamindars themselves. The mansion had huge pillars and had a huge garden in front of it. It was a dilapidated old building and though the construction was solid, it wasn't maintained at all well. Now it must be completely finished. We had it painted — the walls, the pillars, the doors, the windows. It was all levelled up and we made a little path in the garden. Of course, there wasn't any garden or fountain left, so we told our art director [Biren Naug who had worked on three other Guru Dutt productions: *C.I.D.*, *Pyaasa*, and *Chaudhvin ka Chand*] to create the old look; he put up a fountain and plants. We sort of renovated the old *haveli*. There is a shot in the film where Chhote Babu is brought home drunk in the dead of the night and two people carry him in, while Bhoothnath is watching through the window in the servants quarters. The servants quarter was actually part of the main house, so we reconstructed that part of the house, and built two walls and a window.

Sahib Bibi aur Ghulam has many marvellous examples of the confidence with which Murthy and Guru Dutt use lighting to dramatic effect. Jabba sings, *Meri baat rahi mere man main...* (What I wanted to

Baaz was publicised in all the leading film magazines in 1953 but failed to impress critics and audiences

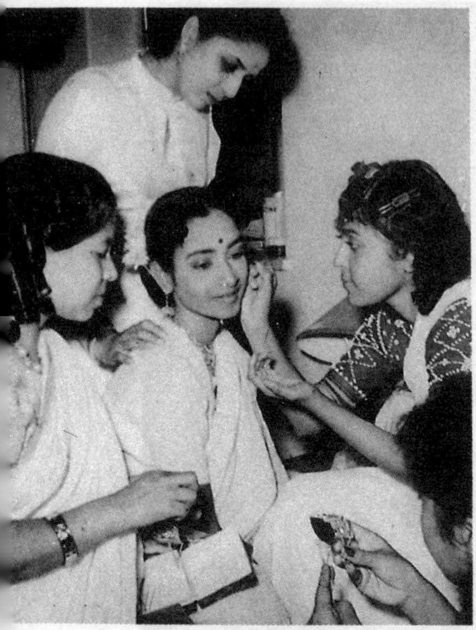

Geeta Bali and friends with
Geeta Roy on her wedding day

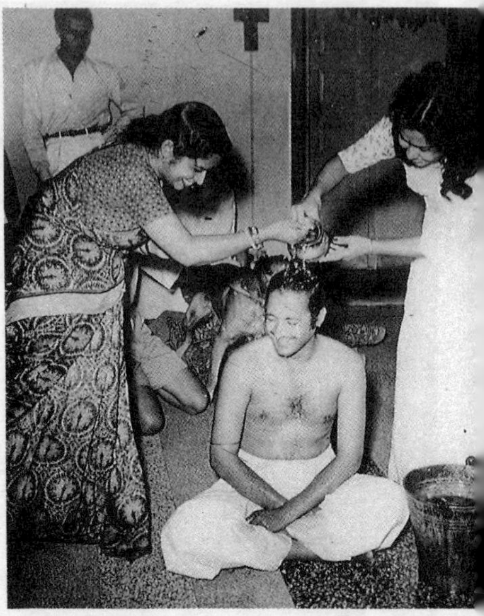

Mrs Arvind Sen and Meena Kapoor
give Guru Dutt his ceremonial bath
before the marriage rituals begin

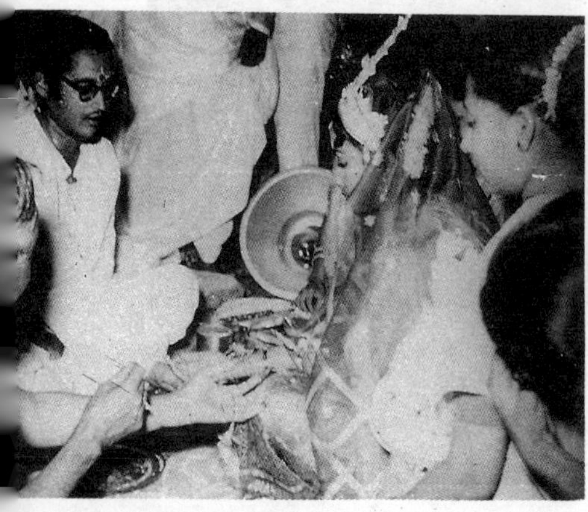

The wedding ceremony held in Bombay
on May 26, 1953

Dev Anand and other friends at Geeta
and Guru Dutt's wedding

Waheeda Rehman as Shanti (*Kaagaz ke Phool*)

Guru Dutt as Sinha and Waheeda Rehman as Shanti (*Kaagaz ke Phool*)

Guru Dutt the film director with audience and studios at his command
(Kaagaz ke Phool)

The director after rejection by his audience *(Kaagaz ke Phool)*

Of all Guru Dutt's films, *Chaudhvin ka Chand* was the most commercially successful

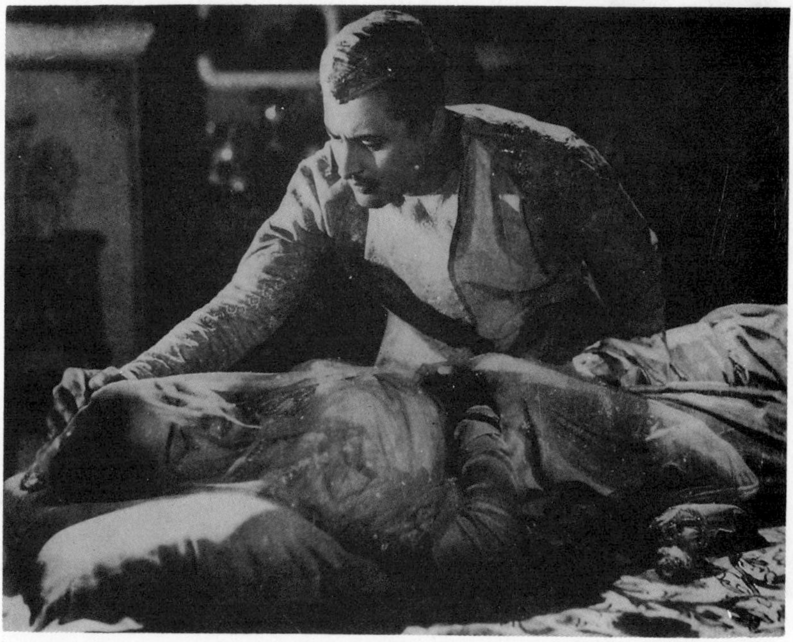

Waheeda Rehman and Guru Dutt (*Chaudhvin ka Chand*)

Friends in cinema and in life, Guru Dutt, Rehman and Johnny Walker
(*Chaudhvin ka Chand*)

Waheeda Rehman as Gulab (*Pyaasa*)

Guru Dutt as Vijay (*Pyaasa*)

Guru Dutt, S.Guruswamy, V.K.Murthy (all facing camera) near Calcutta for the abandoned film 'Gouri'

Geeta Dutt in a publicity still for 'Gouri'

Niranjan,Guru Dutt and V.K.Murthy on location in Simla for the uncompleted 'Raaz'

Guru Dutt and Waheeda Rehman cast in 'Raaz'

Guru Dutt filmed at the Vauhini Studios, Madras (*Kaagaz ke Phool*)

Guru Dutt and Waheeda Rehman filmed at Mehboob Studios, Bombay (*Kaagaz ke Phool*)

Mala Sinha and Guru Dutt during the making of *Baharen Phir Bhi Aayengi*

Guru Dutt and Sadhana in the uncompleted 'Picnic' directed by R.S.Tara

Simi in *Kaneez*, another abandoned film project

Guru Dutt was cast as Majnu in K.Asif's *Love and God*

Geeta Dutt, January 1961 (Photograph: Wolf Suschitzky)

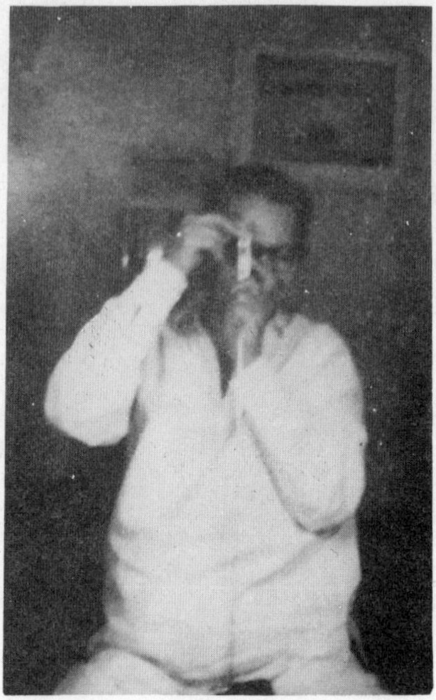

Guru Dutt's self-portrait taken in his Ark Royal flat in Bombay, a few days before he died

Signature

Vasanthi Padukone, Bombay early 1960s

Lalitha Lajmi and Vasanthi Padukone in their Matunga flat, Bombay 1989 (Photograph: Peter Chappell)

Geeta and Guru Dutt with their sons Tarun and Arun, January 1961
(Photograph: Wolf Suschitzky)

The Padukone family gather for a religious ceremony at the Pali Hill house

Rehman and Meena Kumari in song sequence *Na jao saiyan* (*Sahib Bibi aur Ghulam*)

Meena Kumari as Chhoti Bahu and Guru Dutt as Bhoothnath (*Sahib Bibi aur Ghulam*)

Minoo Mumtaz performs in the *haveli* music room (*Sahib Bibi aur Ghulam*)

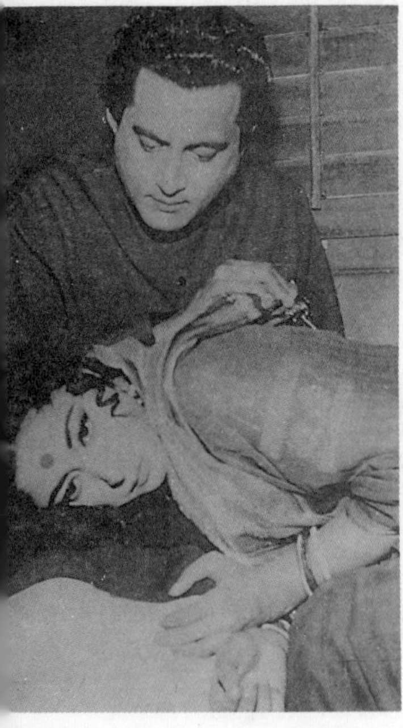

A shot edited out of the final
equence in *Sahib Bibi aur Ghulam*

Waheeda Rehman as Jabba
(*Sahib Bibi aur Ghulam*)

Publicity still with Shyama and Guru Dutt (*Aar Paar*)

Shyama and Johnny enjoy a break on set

Guru Dutt and Shyama on location at the South Indian Garage in Parel, Bombay (*Aar Paar*)

Guru Dutt and Shyama (*Aar Paar*)

say remained in my heart...) in a long-shot: it is early evening and the light is falling on her face. As the camera tracks in towards Jabba, the light vanishes from her face, and darkness engulfs her. In silhouette, she continues with the second line of the song, *Kuchh keh na saki uljhan main* (In the confusion, I could not utter a word). Another well-remembered lighting effect is in the song, *Saaqiya aaj mujhe neend nahin aayegi* (O wine bearer, today sleep shall elude me). Here the lighting in the scene allows the viewer to see only the lead singer (Minoo Mumtaz, comedian Mehmood's sister who was frequently cast in Guru Dutt's films), while the dancers are always seen in shadow as they dance and sing in chorus. The editing of this song is exceptionally exciting and energetic. Brightly-lit shots of twinkling eyes and twirling clothes are juxtaposed with silhouetted figures moving among the pillars of the zamindar's grand music room.

The editing rhythm in the film with its many dissolves and effective use of fades add to its mysterious feel. Editor Y.G. Chawhan worked with Guru Dutt for all his films excepting *Jaal*; Chawhan is proud to observe that the editing in Guru Dutt's films is now studied by students of cinema. When Chawhan came to Bombay from Indore, he had wanted to be an actor, but only managed to work in films as an extra. One of these brief appearances was in Gyan Mukherjee's *Kismet* (1943), in the famous song, *Door hato o duniyawalo*, Chawhan was one of the chorus members.

Y.G. CHAWHAN: I was editing at Navketan with Chetan Anand when I met Guru Dutt. I edited *Neecha Nagar* [1946], *Afsar* [1950], and then *Baazi*. Guru Dutt and I got on very well and he asked me to leave Navketan and join him. When we edited we would run the rushes on the screen, not on the [editing] table. If, for example, there were ten takes, we would select the best one. If you work with a director, you know when you need a close-up, a long shot or a mid-shot. In editing, you learn how long the shot must last. Guru Dutt was a man who would make sure each shot was good. If it wasn't, he'd re-shoot it. Guru Dutt had his own editing room at the studios in Andheri, he had a moviola. After a scene was edited, he would watch it projected on the screen. When we made *Sailaab*, we saw it on the screen. It wasn't very good, so Guru Dutt called Geeta's brother who was the film's producer. Guru Dutt told him not to release the film. The producer [Mukul Roy] said, 'I'll be ruined! ' Guru Dutt told him that he would give him the money but not to release the film.

> For *Sahib Bibi aur Ghulam*, Abrar Alvi sat with me. Abrar worked so hard on that film but he never got any credit. People say it was produced by Guru Dutt so it had to be Guru Dutt's film.

The controversy and ambiguities about who actually directed *Sahib Bibi aur Ghulam* have increased over the years, and were indirectly created by Guru Dutt himself. Because his mental state had become so fragile after the failure of *Kaagaz ke Phool*, and despite his renewed success with *Chaudhvin ka Chand*, the spirit to fight eluded him. Guru Dutt was unwilling to take on the direction of *Sahib Bibi aur Ghulam*, and considered Satyen Bose and Nitin Bose for the task. He finally asked his associate and writer to direct what was to be Alvi's first film. Alvi was sent to Calcutta with a Bengali specialist to visit the palaces of zamindars, to observe their mannerisms and to prepare himself to direct the film. Guru Dutt never denied Alvi's role in the film; nor did he make any counter-claims when *Filmfare*'s Best Director award for 1962 was awarded to Abrar Alvi. It is ironic that Guru Dutt himself never received any awards for the films that he did sign as director. Since *Sahib Bibi aur Ghulam* is deeply imbued with Guru Dutt's style, it is difficult to believe that Guru Dutt, being an experienced director as well as both producer and actor in the film, did not take over its direction. Abrar Alvi has always stated that Guru Dutt did direct the songs in the film, but not the film in its entirety. If this confusion tells us anything at all, it is how little Guru Dutt cared for public recognition at this stage of his life. The stories behind the making of *Sahib Bibi aur Ghulam* reflect a period of darkness in Guru Dutt's personal life: his marriage was more troubled than ever and his relationship with Waheeda Rehman had ended.

During the making of *Sahib Bibi aur Ghulam*, Guru Dutt attempted suicide for the third time. His sister, Lalitha Lajmi, remembers the trauma of those difficult days

> During the filming of the last few scenes in *Sahib Bibi aur Ghulam*, he had taken an overdose of sleeping pills. He was completely cold and we rushed him to Nanavati Hospital. He was in a very, very serious condition. He was in a coma for three days and three nights. In fact, I still remember the day when he came through, it was sometime in the afternoon, and he was shouting and screaming. They had to tie his hands and feet because he had become very aggressive. His first words were to ask for Geeta. I was amazed because there were a lot of differences between them, they were almost separated: but even in those unconscious

moments he was calling out for her and he wanted her to be near him.

CHAPTER FOURTEEN

Lost to Life

After the release of *Sahib Bibi aur Ghulam*, Geeta and Guru Dutt went to Kashmir for a brief holiday with their two sons, Tarun and Arun. Guru Dutt had always wanted a daughter, and was overjoyed when in August 1962, Nina, their third child, was born in Bombay. Relations between Geeta and Guru Dutt seemed repaired for a short while. A year or so later, in the summer of 1963, they decided to pull down their old bungalow in Pali Hill, Bandra, to build an apartment block in its place. This desirable residential suburb of Bombay was in the process of being modernized, and over the years the old-fashioned bungalows were gradually being replaced by high-rise 'luxury' apartment blocks. Following a religious ceremony held by the family at the Pali Hill bungalow, the house was razed to the ground calling to some people's minds the *haveli* ruins in *Sahib Bibi aur Ghulam.* Lalitha Lajmi recalled that Geeta was in fact keen to see the bungalow destroyed because she believed that the house was haunted and that the ghost who lived in the garden tree was destroying their marriage. Many years later, a high-rise apartment block called Sea View Palace was built on the land where Guru Dutt's bungalow once stood.

Guru Dutt and his family moved in 1963 from Pali Hill to the nearby area of Pali Naka where they rented a flat in an apartment block called Ashish. Guru Dutt's younger son, Arun, remembers the days of his childhood with nostalgia:

> Papa was very fond of flying kites, but the Pali Hill house did not have a terrace so he would fly kites at Johnny [Walker] Uncle's house near Carter Road. In those days, there were no sky-scrapers in Pali Hill; our bungalow was the old type of house with slates. I remember that we left Pali Hill in July 1963. We had thought we would be returning to Pali Hill when the construction was done.

There were very heavy rains that year, and there was a leak in the dining room. The dining table that you see here, this very table, was in the old bungalow. When we started moving to smaller and smaller places, we had to keep reducing the size of the table. In those days, it was a huge table with a huge black glass on it. While we were shifting from Pali Hill, the glass slipped and smashed.

We moved to Ashish, which is just opposite Dilip Kumar's house in Bandra, and stayed there for about six months. My parents must have had a big fight and they separated. Papa bought a flat on Peddar Road [in central Bombay], and we moved to a rented place on Hill Road, Bandra. When Papa died, my mother had a nervous breakdown. For nearly three months she could not recognize us. She was very attached to him. She got many offers of remarriage. She said, 'Nothing doing, I'm not changing my surname.'

By early 1964, Guru Dutt had moved out of Ashish to live in Ark Royal on Peddar Road. He lived alone there, looked after by his valet, Ratan, and his cook, Ibrahim. In order to supplement his earnings and to keep his studio running, Guru Dutt acted in four outside productions which were released during 1963/64: *Bahurani* (1963), directed by T. Prakash Rao with Mala Sinha, *Bharosa* (1963), directed by K. Shanker with Asha Parekh, *Suhagan* (1964), directed by K.S. Gopalakrishnan also with Mala Sinha and *Sanjh aur Savera* (1964), directed by Hrishikesh Mukherjee with Meena Kumari. The first three films were shot in Madras and allowed Guru Dutt a brief respite from Bombay; but the films themselves were mediocre and quickly forgotten. During the same period, Guru Dutt was cast in K. Asif's film *Love and God*. K. Asif, whose reputation was built on the spectacular *Mughal-e-Azam* (1960), excelled in making Muslim costume romances. *Love and God*, planned in K. Asif's generous style as another lavish spectacle, was the story of the legendary Arabian lovers, Laila and Majnu. Guru Dutt was cast by his friend Asif as the doomed Majnu and Nimmi as Laila. *Love and God* was almost abandoned when K. Asif himself died in 1971. Asif's wife Akhtar made sure that the film was completed, and it was eventually released in 1986 with Sanjeev Kumar in the role which Guru Dutt was to have played.

ATMARAM: Guru Dutt was a successful actor in his own way. He was commanding a price of about 3 to 5 lakhs: he was paid about 3 lakhs for the South Indian productions, *Bahurani* and *Bharosa*. He had also acted in a film called 'Picnic' opposite Sadhana, sometime in the late fifties. The film was being produced by R.S. Tara, but it was shelved [one song was shot and shows Guru Dutt's own filming style]. Guru Dutt was also working in K. Asif's *Love and God.*

My wife and I had lived peacefully in London for three years. Then we came back to Bombay. Suddenly, I'd get a telephone call at midnight: Guru Dutt wants me or Guru Dutt is in hospital or Guru Dutt has taken sleeping pills. One day, he said to me, 'Come and stay with me.' Sometimes he used to say that an astrologer had predicted that he would go mad at the age of thirty-two and he believed it. I think it really was true. He had started drinking heavily, but never when he was shooting. He was a strict disciplinarian as far as work was concerned, but totally undisciplined in his personal life.

Guru Dutt decided to make a film in the 'Arabian Nights' style called 'Kaneez', sometime in 1962/63. The film was to be shot in colour with Simi and Randhir in the lead roles. I think some shooting did commence but Guru Dutt decided to drop the project. Simi was furious and complained to the Cine Artists Association; K. Asif was the arbitrator and finally we paid every penny to her.

In April 1964, Guru Dutt went on a hunting trip in Madhya Pradesh with Tarun and Arun, together with Johnny Walker and Guruswamy. Though 'Kaneez' had been dropped, Guru Dutt was so impressed by Raj Kapoor's *Sangam,* released in 1964, that he often talked of making a colour film as soon as he could. By this time, however, it was clear to Guru Dutt that he would not be able to make the kind of films that really interested him. Despite the enormous effort that he had made in *Kaagaz ke Phool* during his lifetime, *Pyaasa* still remained the only serious work to be acclaimed by critics and audiences. He no longer believed that he could repeat that success. In his article, 'Classics and Cash' in *Celluloid*, Guru Dutt describes his isolation:

> In the formula-ridden film world of ours one who ventures to go off the beaten track is condemned to the definition which Matthew Arnold used for Shelley: 'an angel beating wings in a void.' I believe one who is out to go against the winds has to be prepared for bouquets as well as brickbats, for triumphs as well as heart-breaks, whether or not one makes a classic or collects the cash. It is this baffling unpredictability that gives the edge to the thrill of movie-making.

In 1963/64, the production of *Baharen Phir Bhi Aayengi* (The Spring Will Return) was started. The film was based on the 1937 film *President*, also known under the titles *Didi* and *Badi Bahen*. *President*, a classic New Theatres' film, was directed by Nitin Bose with K.L. Saigal and Leela Desai in the lead roles. The original background of a 1930s textile mill was made more contemporary by situating this new version in the offices of a national newspaper called *Jagriti* (Awakening). Guru Dutt was cast in the lead role of Jitendra, a journalist who exposes corruption and is subsequently fired. The newspaper owner, Anita (Mala Sinha), later reinstates him and falls in love with him. Though Jitendra has great regard for her, he is in love with Anita's younger sister, Sunita (Tanuja), whom he meets by chance. A further love triangle is introduced as a colleague, Varma (Rehman), is in love with Anita but does not admit it. Chunilal (Johnny Walker), the newspaper photographer, provides the comedy in a tale that ends tragically with the heroine Anita going insane and dying.

Guru Dutt asked Shahid Lateef to direct *Baharen Phir Bhi Aayengi*, and O.P. Nayyar was persuaded to compose its music. It was during the recording of the film's score that Guru Dutt was said to comment that O. P. Nayyar composed feelings not words. A number of lyricists including Kaifi Azmi and Anjaan wrote for *Baharen Phir Bhi Aayengi*. The film's most famous song, *Aap ke haseen rukh pe aaj naya noor hai* (Your beautiful face glows today with a new light), written by Anjaan, was picturized by Guru Dutt. The song was loved by everyone who saw it, as Guru Dutt had filmed it with his usual flair. In the role of the heroine's sister, Sunita, Guru Dutt cast young Tanuja, who belonged to a distinguished family of actresses starting with her mother Shobhana Samarth, and followed by her elder sister, Nutan.

TANUJA: I did see the film *President* and was quite intrigued by it; what especially interested me was the relationship between the two sisters. Guru Dutt chose me and stuck with me. I signed the film in 1962; we worked for almost a year between 1963-64. I was not a very dedicated actress. That used to bug him no end. He would ring up my mother and say, 'Don't tell her I told you but....' We shared some very good moments. We both loved to read, we talked about everything under the sun. When he heard that his friend, art director Biren Naug had died [in 1964], he was very upset. He cancelled the shooting that day.

A lot of people said that Guru Dutt had a terrible temper and that he was suicidal. I never saw that side of him. He always laughed with me; everyone wanted me on the set because I made him laugh. In fact, one day his driver Ayub said, 'Sahib is in a very bad mood, the workers want you to come.' Guru Dutt once returned from shooting in Madras, and bought a doll for his daughter, Nina. She came to see him at Guru Dutt's studios; I remember the kid running down the corridor and he picking her up and twirling her around — she was the light of his life. He taught me never to make distinctions between people, to treat everyone as equals. He was very close to his team and they adored the ground he walked on. He had this intensity which he was able to infuse in other artists. As an actor, you end up reflecting the director. It's not *you* who is acting but you're acting *his* way. I think we shot about 11 reels together.

V.K. Murthy was working in Madras at the time and encouraged his long-time assistant K.G. Prabhakar to take over the photography of *Baharen Phir Bhi Aayengi*:

Actually, I had given a break to my assistant in that film. I was working on two films at the time in Madras including *Suraj* (1966). T. Prakash Rao was the director of *Suraj*. He was a popular director and one day he asked me, 'Do you know how I learned to be a director? I said, 'You worked with Mr L.V. Prasad.' He answered, 'I learned direction after seeing *Pyaasa* — thirty-six times.' Some scenes of *Suraj* were being filmed at Mehboob Studios in Bombay and Guru Dutt sent word to me there to come and shoot some scenes of *Baharen* after my day's shoot. I did photograph some scenes in the film with Mala Sinha and Johnny Walker's song [*Suno suno Miss Chatterji mere dil ki matter-ji*].

Guru Dutt wouldn't speak of his troubles to others. Once during the filming of *Chaudhvin ka Chand*, we were talking and he said, 'Now I have name and money but I'm not interested in it. I wonder what meaning life really has. *Duniya agar mil bhi jaaye to kya hai* [refrain from the *Pyaasa* song, 'If I gain the world, what of it?']. What else is there to life? People say I make good films. So what?' While he was making *Baharen*, he called me to his flat in Peddar Road. At that time, Geeta and he were separated and Guru Dutt was all alone in his flat with Ratan, his attendant. Ratan was the only one who could control him — to a certain extent. We sat quietly for a long time and then he said, 'The family has separated, you went away to Madras, I am alone, only Ratan is here with me. How much do they pay you in Madras? I'll give you the money they've advanced, return it to them. Don't go back to Madras.' I realized that something had gone wrong with him.

In early October, 1964, a reporter from *The Times of India* visited the sets of *Baharen Phir Bhi Aayengi* which was being shot at Guru Dutt's studios in Andheri. Guru Dutt asked the journalist if he could visit the offices of *The Times* the following week in order to make sure his portrayal of a newspaper concern would be accurate. That visit was never to take place. On Saturday, October 10, 1964, Guru Dutt took his own life. He was discovered by his servant Ratan in the Ark Royal flat. The post-mortem report stated that he had died early that morning. Guru Dutt was in the thirty-ninth year of his life and the deep psychological disturbances that had provoked his repeated attempts at suicide finally led to his death from an overdose of sleeping tablets. Though he did not voice his feelings, his suicide reflected the profound nature of his depression and grief. The fame and success that he had achieved in his short life were clearly insufficient to alleviate his inner turmoil; though he had creativity and talent in large measure they failed to contain him.

During the making of *Baharen Phir Bhi Aayengi*, he drank and smoked heavily and no one had any real influence over his habits. Each day passed and though his family knew of his depressions, no one suspected the seriousness of his mental instability.

DEVI DUTT: On the 9th of October, I had lunch with Guru Dutt and Tanuja on the sets of *Baharen*. I was making ad films in those days. Guru Dutt sent his driver to get the children from home and they came and they started flying kites. I was fond of cricket and there was a match between Australia and India. He gave me tickets for the next day's match, and then he asked me to go with him and the children to Chiragh Din [boutique] in Colaba. Guru Dutt liked ready-made shirts and he started shopping there. It's a very expensive place and he bought lots of clothes for the children and bought me two pants and two shirts. The children went home and I went with him to his Peddar Road flat. He asked me if I wanted an omelette, and prepared one. He didn't have a telephone in the flat so we went to the neighbours' on the ground floor and we called Mala Sinha in Madras. He spoke to her and went up again. Around 8 p.m., he asked me to call Mr Asif. I did and Asif Sahib said, 'I'll come there at 10 p.m., not now.'

Guru Dutt was in a very good mood that day. At 9.30 p.m. he asked me to call Geeta [at her mother's house in Santa Cruz] and tell her that he wanted the children. I spoke to my sister-in-law. She said, 'What nonsense! Why are you calling now? The children were with him all afternoon. I will send them tomorrow. Tell him I won't send them now, they're sleeping.' I came up and told him it is not possible for the children to come. At the time, Guru Dutt was drinking. He told me, 'Now, you can go.' As I was about to leave, Abrar Sahib arrived. Guru Dutt was planning to build a big house and he showed Abrar the model of the house. They were talking and I asked Guru Dutt in Konkani, 'Can I go?' That was my last glimpse of him.

For the greater part of 1964, Abrar Alvi had been working in Madras and only returned to Bombay in September of that year. Realizing that Guru Dutt was particularly lonely, Alvi had lived for some weeks with him at Ark Royal. In early October, Abrar Alvi returned to his home in Juhu but most evenings were spent working on the script of *Baharen* at Guru Dutt's flat. Quite naturally, Abrar Alvi was with Guru Dutt on the evening of October 9. Guru Dutt's tax consultant, Mr Gole, joined them for dinner while Alvi was busy discussing the last scene of *Baharen Phir Bhi Aayengi*. In the last scene of the film, the heroine — overcome with loneliness — has gone insane and has a heart attack and dies.

ABRAR ALVI: Guru Dutt had started drinking very early that evening. I was busy writing. He sat down and talked of many things, some crazy things too. He talked of a friend who was in an asylum and who had written to him. Guru Dutt said, 'You can't tell by reading his letter that he is crazy. Sometimes I think I'll go insane.' I said, 'What are you saying, why would you go mad?' He was very, very disturbed. I was with him until 1 a.m. He didn't open up. And if I knew he was going to do that mad thing, I would never have left him. He sat with me at the dining-table, but he didn't eat. Finally he said, 'Abrar, if you don't mind, I'd like to retire.'

I gave the scene that I had written to Ratan and then I left. Later on I heard that Guru Dutt had got up around 3.30 a.m. and had woken Ratan and asked him, 'Where is Abrar Sahib?' Ratan told him that I had left after dinner and he asked if he should telephone me. Guru Dutt said, 'No, let it be.' Ratan then asked if he could make him a drink. He said, 'No. Give me the bottle.' He took the bottle into his room and locked the door behind him. He used to take sleeping pills — Sonarils. So he must have had a lethal dose. The post-mortem results stated that he died around 5.30 to 6.00 a.m. on Saturday 10, October, 1964.

During the evening of October 9, Guru Dutt had also rung Raj Kapoor and fixed an appointment to see him the next day. In an article published in *Filmfare* (October 30, 1964), Abrar Alvi wrote that during that same evening, Guru Dutt was restless and had told Ratan to telephone O.P. Nayyar as well, but Nayyar was not available. On the day that Guru Dutt died, his sister, Lalitha Lajmi, had organized a musical evening in her home and had hoped that Guru Dutt would attend. She recalls:

We had invited guests to come to our home for a sitar recital by Abdul Haleem Khan on the 10th of October, so I had gone a few days earlier to invite Guru Dutt. He said, 'Lalli, I'm not coming for the party — I feel lost when I'm in a crowd. I'd prefer to come on a day when we are just by ourselves.' He was very fond of pickles and my mother had sent a large jar. He said, 'Come and join me for dinner, let's eat mother's pickles.' Those were the last few words he said to me. The day he passed away, I didn't know about it. About 12 o'clock one of his assistants rang saying, 'Guru Dutt is no more.' I rushed to Ark Royal, Geeta was there sobbing, my mother was there. The first person to arrive at Peddar Road was Dev Anand. Then all the actors came, the entire film industry was there.

Guru Dutt was lying in a peculiar position when he died. His leg was lifted, it was as though he was about to get up from the bed. There was an unfinished Hindi novel by his bed-side, the lights were on. It was like a frozen moment. They had found him at 10.30 in the morning. Geeta had called and asked his servant to break open the door. Later his body was taken for post-mortem and very late that evening, the funeral took place. He was dressed in a dark suit when he was taken away. His body looked so fresh excepting a tinge of blue in his ears that gave the feeling of death, otherwise he was looking very, very fresh. Just ten minutes before his body was going for cremation, Waheeda arrived. She had been shooting in Madras. It's a big question whether it was suicide or whether it had been heart failure in his sleep. One still doesn't know, but probably it was intentional.

Waheeda Rehman and Johnny Walker were in Madras when they received the news, and rushed back to Bombay in time for the funeral. According to custom, the funeral rites are supposed to be performed by the eldest son, but because Tarun was so young, Atmaram performed the last rites at Sonapur crematorium. The cortege reached Sonapur on Queen's Road at around 8.10 p.m. Raj Kapoor, who had helped with all the Coroner's formalities, referred sadly to the previous day's telephone call and how Guru Dutt and he had planned to meet. K. Asif, who had just come out of hospital, attended the funeral with his right arm in a sling. Meena Kumari, Prithviraj Kapoor and Nargis were among the many mourners. Nargis recalled that Geeta had had a strange premonition the night before Guru Dutt died, and that was why she had insisted that Ratan break open Guru Dutt's bedroom door.

Every newspaper and film magazine in India carried the news of Guru Dutt's suicide. The *Filmfare* issue of October 30, 1964, included a lead article on Guru Dutt titled 'Khuda, Maut aur Ghulam'(God, Death and Slave) in which his friends and family shocked by his death, expressed themselves as best as they could. Kaifi Azmi wrote a poem in tribute to Guru Dutt that was featured in *Filmfare*'s cover article; the poem *Rehne ko sadaa dehr mein aata nahin koi, tum jaise gaye aise bhi jaata nahin koi* (No one comes to stay for ever, but no one leaves as you did), aptly voiced Azmi's own sadness.

KAIFI AZMI: Guru Dutt's death affected me personally. I wrote a poem to him. I still think of him a lot. The reason why he didn't succeed as much as he could have done was that he was born ahead of his times. He made films at a very young age and if he had lived longer, he would have created much more. He used to work very hard, and was very demanding in his work. He would often talk about the kind of films he would have liked to make, and the shape that Indian films should take. I think a lot about what he used to say. He was not able to achieve what he wanted. He did not have enough time.

When *Baharen Phir Bhi Aayengi* was finally released in 1966, it opened with a still photograph of Guru Dutt accompanied by the caption: 'Presented as Guru Dutt's last offering.' Even though the film was almost entirely re-shot with Dharmendra replacing Guru Dutt, a few scenes from the original shooting were kept in the final version and bear Guru Dutt's mark. It is more than likely that he had personally filmed the song *Vo hanske mile humse, hum pyaar samajh baithe* (He met me smilingly and I mistook it for love) sung by Asha Bhosle for Mala Sinha. The juxtaposition of light and shade, moving crane shots that end on a close-up and tracking shots used for dramatic and emotional effect in the song evoke the familiar mood that Guru Dutt and Murthy had so often created together.

V.K.MURTHY: On the day that he died, I was in Bangalore. The moment I got the telephone call, I was completely down in my mood. I couldn't even reply, 'What, what has happened? How could it happen? ' After some time, maybe you can call it selfishness, I had thought I lost a good person, and also my technique. That's exactly what happened. He had a jeweller's eye. Just as a jeweller can find out which is the best diamond, he had the knack of extracting the best from a person. That's how he has been very successful in having a good team of actors, technicians, music directors, art directors. He had that knack. It's something remarkable.

That team spirit that Guru Dutt had inspired faded with time, and few members of his closely-knit group ever worked together again. Though many of Guru Dutt's most preferred artists such as Waheeda Rehman, Rehman or Johnny Walker appeared in several other films, their best work has always been associated with Guru Dutt.

JOHNNY WALKER: There are those who make films for the masses and there are those who make films for the gentry. Guru Dutt was a director whose films were liked by the gentry *and* the masses. That was his greatest quality. He was a top technician and a very good man.

After Guru Dutt's death, Atmaram and S. Guruswamy kept Guru Dutt's company going, and their first task was the completion of *Baharen Phir Bhi Aayengi*. The film did not do well at the box-office. A few years later, Atmaram began directing feature films: some fared well and others bombed.

ATMARAM: The business of filmmaking makes us all insecure. Guru Dutt could be regarded as eccentric, difficult to live with, difficult to work with, highly intuitive. Sometimes he would go into his shell and not be available to anyone. He died at the age of thirty-nine. I like to remember him as one remembers the poets Shelley, Keats or Byron. Guru Dutt made a few films but he seems to have left such a mark. I could never have imagined when working with him that people would remember him so long and so well. With all works of art that have lasted, it is because the artist concerned has put everything that he has got in his personality into his work. That's what Guru Dutt did.

Guru Dutt himself could not have predicted the impact that he would have in time; not only in India but in many parts of Europe, his films would be seen and re-seen. Death has indeed brought the kind of recognition that echoes his own feelings suggested in *Pyaasa* — that a dead artist is more greatly valued. Some fifteen years after his death, a revival of Guru Dutt's work began. This revival had a modest beginning, but significantly, it coincided with an increased academic and critical interest in the study of popular Indian cinema. Firoze Rangoonwalla had written a monograph on Guru Dutt in 1973 and sporadic morning screenings of Guru Dutt's films in Indian cities, particularly in Delhi and Bombay, assured distributors that he still had a dedicated following. Increased interest in Guru Dutt's films then began in the late seventies and early eighties when a French critic, Henri Micciollo, wrote an excellent study of his films. Micciollo, who worked at the Alliance Francaise in Bombay during the seventies, happened to attend a morning screening of *Pyaasa*. The film was un-subtitled but Micciollo was deeply moved and intrigued by both the film and its director. Micciollo's writings introduced Guru Dutt's work to the West long before Europeans even had the chance to see his films for themselves. In India, critics and film scholars began to write about Guru Dutt and his work.

In the early 1980s, a Guru Dutt retrospective was organized in Bombay by his sons Tarun and Arun with the help of the film distributor L. Lachman. Around the same time, international film festivals held in France, Italy and America highlighted the work of Indian directors of the fifties, and among the many films shown, Guru Dutt's work shone brightly. Some of his films were also shown on British television, and *Pyaasa* and *Kaagaz ke Phool* were released in Paris cinemas. The number of Guru Dutt's followers continue to grow moved by his talent and personal tragedy. A Japanese librarian who had seen *Pyaasa* in a 1988 festival of Indian cinema held in Tokyo wrote: 'Guru Dutt's films made me realize that a film is a world in itself. If *Pyaasa* was not in the selection, I would never have been as committed as I am now to Indian cinema.'

The connection between Guru Dutt's screen personae and his own person has grown so close that he lives on in his films as each work seems to tell us something more about him. As Preetam, Vijay or Suresh Sinha vanish behind a dark pillar, out of the light and into the darkness, Guru Dutt too eluded those who were close to him. Recountings of his silent ways and his introversion remind us that cinema was his way of reaching out.

RAJ KHOSLA: You couldn't read through Guru Dutt, but I read one thing about him, even in those days, that he was really lost — lost in filmmaking, but lost to life.

Select Bibliography

BANERJEE, Shampa: 'Guru Dutt' in *Profiles; Five Filmmakers from India*. Festival of India, USA, 1985-86.

CHATTERJEE, Partha: 'Remembering Guru Dutt'. *Cinemaya* 13, 1991.

COOPER, Darius: 'The Hindi Film Song and Guru Dutt'. *East-West Film Journal* 2 (2), 1988.

JHA, Ratna Dhar: 'Homage to Five Masters'. New Delhi, Directorate of Film Festivals, 1984.

KHOPKAR, Arun: *Guru Dutt: Teen Anki Shokantika*. [In Marathi.] Poona, Granthali, 1985.

KRISHNA, Lalitha: 'The Great Romantics: an Assessment of Guru Dutt's Oeuvre'. *Filmfare*, March 1987.

LAJMI, Lalitha: 'Unfinished symphony'. *Filmfare*, February 1995.

MASUD, Iqbal: 'The Legend of Guru Dutt'. *The Illustrated Weekly of India*, November 27-December 3, 1983.

MICCIOLLO, Henri: *Guru Dutt* [In French.] Paris, Avant-Scene, 1976.

MUJAWAR, Isak: *Guru Dutt, Ek Asanta Kalabanta*. [In Marathi.] Poona, Srividya Prakasana, 1985.

PADUKONE, Vasanthi: 'My son Guru Dutt'. *Imprint*, April 1979.

RANGOONWALLA, Firoze: *Guru Dutt, 1925-1965: a Monograph*. Poona, National Film Archives of India, 1973.

Screen, October 13 1989. [Special issue on Guru Dutt.]

Filmography

1945

LAKHRANI (aka LAKHARANI)

Production concern: Prabhat Film Company

Lyrics: Qamar Jalalabadi

Music: Krishna Rao

Director: Vishram Bedekar

Cast: Durga Khote, Monica Desai, Sapru, Ramsingh

Guru Dutt worked as assistant director and also acted as Lachman.

1946

HUM EK HAIN

Production concern: Prabhat Film Company

Lyrics: P.L. Santoshi

Music: Husnlal-Bhagatram

Director: P.L. Santoshi

Cast: Dev Anand, Durga Khote, Rehana, Kamla Kotnis, Rehman, Ramsingh

Guru Dutt worked as assistant director, dance director and also appeared in a brief role.

1947

MOHAN

Production concern: Famous Pictures

Lyrics: Qamar Jalalabadi

Music: Husnlal-Bhagatram

Director: Anadinath Banerji

Cast: Hemavati, Dev Anand, Alaka, Vimla Vasistha

Guru Dutt worked as assistant director.

1949

GIRLS SCHOOL

Production concern: Lokmanya Productions

Lyrics: Pradeep

Music: C. Ramchandra & Anil Biswas

Director: Amiya Chakravarty

Cast: Geeta Bali, Sohan, Shashikala, Sajjan, Mangla, Ramsingh

Guru Dutt worked as first assistant director.

1950

SANGRAM

Production concern: Bombay Talkies

Story & screenplay: Gyan Mukherjee

Dialogues: V. Gaur

Dances: Narendra Sharma

Photography: Josef Wirsching

Lyrics: Vrajendra Gaur, Raja Mehndi, Santoshi

Music: C. Ramchandra

Director: Gyan Mukherjee

Cast: Ashok Kumar, Nalini Jaywant, Nawab, Sajjan, Tiwari, Ramsingh, Shashiraj, Baby Tabassum

Guru Dutt worked as assistant director.

1951

BAAZI (The Gamble)

Production concern: Navketan

Story: Guru Dutt & Balraj Sahni

Screenplay & dialogue: Balraj Sahni

Art direction: G.L. Jadhav

Dances: Zohra Sehgal

Editing: Y.G. Chawhan

Photography: V. Ratra

Lyrics: Sahir Ludhianvi

Music: S.D. Burman

Director: Guru Dutt

Cast: Dev Anand (Madan), Geeta Bali (Nina), K.N. Singh (Rajani's father), Mehmood, Badruddin, and introducing Kalpana Kartik (Rajani) and Roopa Varman (Roopa)

Madan is a small-time gambler who turns to crime in order to pay for the treatment of his ailing sister. Dancer Nina is in love with Madan but he has chosen a young doctor, Rajani, instead. Owner of a notorious night-club, Rajani's father tries to have Madan framed for murder.

1952

JAAL (The Net)

Production concern: Filmarts

Producer: T.R. Fatehchand

Story & screenplay: Guru Dutt

Dialogues: M.A. Lateef

Art Director: V.Y. Jadav Rao

Editing: J.S. Diwadkar

Dances: Prof. K.S. More

Photography: V.K. Murthy

Lyrics: Sahir Ludhianvi

Music: S.D. Burman

Director: Guru Dutt

Cast: Dev Anand (Tony), Geeta Bali (Maria), Purnima (Lisa), K.N. Singh (Carlo), Ramsingh (Simon), Rasheed (Police Inspector)

Tony, a ruthless smuggler and his partner, Lisa, have taken refuge in a small fishing village to escape the police. Tony nets the beautiful Maria who falls in love with him. Maria finally succeeds in persuading Tony to repent.

1953

BAAZ (The Falcon)

Production concern: H.G. Films

Producer: Miss Haridarshan

Production Executive: S. Guruswamy

Story & screenplay: Guru Dutt

Dialogue: L.C. Bismil & Sarshar Sailani

Editor: Y.G. Chawhan

Dances: Vinod Chopra

Art direction: V.Y. Jadhav

Photography: V.K. Murthy

Lyrics: Majrooh Sultanpuri

Music: O.P. Nayyar

Director: Guru Dutt

Cast: Geeta Bali (Nisha), Guru Dutt (Prince Ravi), Kuldip Kaur (Rosita), K.N. Singh (General Barbosa), Ramsingh, Sulochana Devi, Jaswant, Johnny Walker

A high-seas adventure set in a 16th century kingdom on the Malabar Coast. The Portuguese are the invaders while Nisha, forced to become a pirate queen, leads the revolt against the aggressors with Prince Ravi. Conventional costume drama in which good triumphs over evil.

1954

AAR PAAR (This side or the other aka Heads or Tails)

Production concern: Guru Dutt Productions

Production Executive: S. Guruswamy

Screenplay: Nabendu Ghosh

Dialogues: Abrar Alvi

Editor: Y.G. Chawhan

Dances: Surya Kumar

Art direction: D.K. Warrior & Hirabai

Photography: V.K. Murthy

Lyrics: Majrooh Sultanpuri

Music: O.P. Nayyar

Director: Guru Dutt

Cast: Shyama (Nikki), Guru Dutt (Kalu Birju), Jagdish Sethi (Nikki's father, Lalaji), Johnny Walker (Rustom), Jagdeep (Elaichi), Shakila (Rita)

Taxi-driver Kalu is released from prison after serving a short sentence for speeding. Down on his luck, he finds work in a garage as mechanic where he falls in love with Nikki, the garage-owner's daughter. When Nikki's father discovers their romancing, he throws Kalu out. Kalu joins a band of crooks, and when he proves himself to be worthy, wins Nikki's hand.

1955

MR & MRS 55

Production concern: Guru Dutt Films Ltd.

Production-in-charge: S. Guruswamy

Dialogues: Abrar Alvi

Art Director: D.R. Jadhav

Dances: Surya Kumar

Photography: V.K. Murthy

Lyrics: Majrooh Sultanpuri

Music: O.P. Nayyar

Director: Guru Dutt

Cast: Madhubala (Anita), Guru Dutt (Preetam), Lalitha Pawar (Sita Devi), Johnny Walker (Johnny), Uma Devi (Lilly D'Silva), Yasmin (Julie), Kumkum

Young Anita must be married before her 21st birthday in order to inherit a large fortune. Preetam seems the ideal 'hired husband', the only difficulty being that he is genuinely in love with Anita. Despite Sita Devi's many ploys to keep them apart, Preetam and Anita are reunited at last.

1956

C.I.D.

Production concern: Guru Dutt Films Ltd.

Producer: Guru Dutt

Screenplay & dialogues: Inder Raj Anand

Dances: Zohra Sehgal

Art director: G.V. Divkar & Biren Naug

Editor: Y.G. Chawhan

Photography: V.K. Murthy

Lyrics: Majrooh Sultanpuri

Music: O.P. Nayyar

Director: Raj Khosla

Cast: Dev Anand, Shakila, Johnny Walker, K.N. Singh, Kumkum, Uma Devi, and introducing Waheeda Rehman

A crime thriller with Dev Anand in the role of Inspector Shekhar of the Criminal Investigation Department.

1956

SAILAAB (The Flood)

Production concern: Emar Films

Producer: Mukul Roy

Lyrics: Majrooh Sultanpuri, Shailendra & Hasrat Jaipuri

Music: Mukul Roy

Director: Guru Dutt

Cast: Abhi Bhattacharya, Geeta Bali, Smriti Biswas, Bipin Gupta, Ramsingh, Helen, Uma Devi

A love story in which the hero suffers from amnesia.

1957

PYAASA (The Thirsting One, aka The Thirsty One)
Production concern: Guru Dutt Films Pvt. Ltd.
Production-in-charge: S. Guruswamy
Dialogues: Abrar Alvi
Art Director: Biren Naug
Editor: Y.G. Chawhan
Dances: Surya Kumar
Photography: V.K. Murthy
Lyrics: Sahir Ludhianvi
Music: S.D. Burman
Director: Guru Dutt
Cast: Mala Sinha (Meena), Guru Dutt (Vijay), Waheeda Rehman (Gulab), Rehman (Mr Ghosh), Johnny Walker (Abdul Sattar), Kumkum, Shyam, Mehmood, Leela Misra, Uma Devi
The first of Guru Dutt's masterpieces, the film tells the story of a poet struggling to find recognition in a materialistic world in which only social outcastes are his true friends.

1958

12 O'CLOCK
Production concern: Sippy Films Pvt Ltd
Producer: G.P. Sippy
Story & screenplay: Pramod Chakravorty
Dialogues: Tanvir Faroqui
Photography: V.K. Murthy
Lyrics: Majrooh Sultanpuri
Music: O.P. Nayyar
Director: Pramod Chakravorty
Cast: Guru Dutt (Ajoy Kumar), Waheeda Rehman (Bani Chowdhury), Shashikala, Rehman, Johnny Walker
Bani, escaping her oppressive family, gets a job in a law firm where she meets and falls in love with Ajoy, her young colleague. Bani is framed for murder and Ajoy comes to her rescue.

1959

KAAGAZ KE PHOOL (Paper Flowers)

Production concern: Guru Dutt Films Pvt. Ltd

Screenplay & dialogues: Abrar Alvi

Editor: Y.G. Chawhan

Art Director: M.R. Achrekar

Production-in-charge: S. Guruswamy

Photography (Cinemascope): V.K. Murthy

Lyrics: Kaifi Azmi

Music: S.D. Burman

Producer/Director: Guru Dutt

Cast: Waheeda Rehman (Shanti), Guru Dutt (Suresh Sinha), Baby Naaz (Pammi), Johnny Walker (Rakesh, aka Rocky), Minoo Mumtaz (Julie), Mahesh Kaul (Sir B.B. Verma), Veena (Bina),

Suresh Sinha is a celebrated film director who is estranged from his wife and daughter. He falls in love with his 'discovery' Shanti whom he grooms to act in films. Sinha's career soon declines and he realises the ephemeral nature of fame and success.

1960

CHAUDHVIN KA CHAND (Fourteenth Day of the Moon aka Full Moon)

Production concern: Guru Dutt Films Pvt. Ltd

Producer: Guru Dutt

Production-in-charge: S. Guruswamy

Screenplay & dialogues: Saghir Usmani

Art director: Biren Naug

Editor: Y.G. Chawhan

Photography: Nariman A. Irani

Lyrics: Shakeel Badayuni

Music: Ravi

Director: M. Sadiq

Cast: Waheeda Rehman (Jamila), Guru Dutt (Aslam), Rehman (Nawab), Johnny Walker (Shaida), Minoo Mumtaz, Uma Devi

Mistaken identity leads to tragedy in this love triangle set in a Muslim milieu. The film is in black and white but includes two song sequences in colour.

1962

SAHIB BIBI AUR GHULAM (Master, Mistress and Slave)

Production concern: Guru Dutt Films Pvt. Ltd.

Producer: Guru Dutt

Based on a novel by: Bimal Mitra

Dialogues: Abrar Alvi & Bimal Mitra

Editor: Y.G. Chawhan

Art director: Biren Naug

Photography: V.K. Murthy

Lyrics: Shakeel Badayuni

Music: Hemant Kumar

Director: Abrar Alvi

Cast: Meena Kumari (Chhoti Bahu), Guru Dutt (Bhoothnath), Rehman (Chhote Babu), Waheeda Rehman (Jabba), Nazir Hussein (Suvinay Babu), Dhumal (Bansi), Sapru (Manjhle Babu), Minoo Mumtaz (dancer)

Through the eyes of Bhoothnath, a simple but educated villager who comes to Calcutta, unfolds the story of a Bengali zamindar family at the turn of the twentieth century. At the heart of the narrative is the tragic Chhoti Bahu.

1963

BAHURANI

Production concern: Meena Pictures, Madras

Dialogue: Inder Raj Anand

Photography: Marcus Bartley

Lyrics: Sahir Ludhianvi

Music: C. Ramchandra

Director: T. Prakash Rao

Cast: Guru Dutt, Mala Sinha, Feroz Khan, Shyama, Agha, Lalita Pawar

A family drama with a virtuous young bride who is tricked into marrying the landlord's simple-minded son.

1963

BHAROSA

Production concern: Vasu Films, Madras

Producer: N.V. Menon

Story: M.S. Solaimalai

Screenplay: J. Sitharaman

Photography: Thambu

Dialogue & lyrics: Rajinder Krishan
Music: Ravi
Director: K. Shankar
Cast: Guru Dutt, Asha Parekh, Mehmood, Shobha Khote

1964
SAANJH AUR SAVERA
Production concern: S.J. Films
Producer: Sevantilal Shah
Story & dialogue: Jagdish Kanwal
Photography: Jaywant Pathare
Lyrics: Shailendra & Hasrat Jaipuri
Music: Shanker-Jaikishan
Director: Hrishikesh Mukherjee
Cast: Meena Kumari, Guru Dutt, Mehmood, Shobha Khote, Manmohna Krishna

1964
SUHAGAN
Production concern: A.L.S. Productions, Madras
Lyrics: Hasrat Jaipuri
Music: Madan Mohan
Director: K.S. Gopalakrishnan
Cast: Guru Dutt, Mala Sinha, Feroz Khan, Nazir Hussein

Film projects shelved by Guru Dutt at various stages of production include:

PROFESSOR
RAAZ
GOURI
EK TUKU CHHUAA (a Bengali language film)
KANEEZ (film planned in colour)

Unfinished films as actor:

BAHAREN PHIR BHI AAYENGI. Produced by Guru Dutt Films Pvt Ltd, directed by Shahid Lateef. Guru Dutt was later replaced by Dharmendra.

LOVE AND GOD. Produced & directed by K. Asif. Guru Dutt in the role of Majnu was later replaced by Sanjeev Kumar.